The Beginner's Guide to *Mathematica*®

Version 2

The Beginner's Guide to *Mathematica*®
Version 2

Theodore W. Gray
Wolfram Research, Inc.

Jerry Glynn
MathWare, The Math Program

ADDISON-WESLEY PUBLISHING COMPANY

Reading, Massachusetts • Menlo Park, California • New York
Don Mills, Ontario • Wokingham, England • Amsterdam • Bonn
Sydney • Singapore • Tokyo • Madrid • San Juan • Milan • Paris

Many of the designations used by manufacturers and sellers to distinguish their products are claimed as trademarks. Where those designations appear in this book, and Addison-Wesley was aware of a trademark claim, the designations have been printed in initial caps or all caps.

Library of Congress Cataloging-in-Publication Data
Gray, Theodore W.
    The beginner's guide to Mathematica / Theodore W. Gray, Jerry Glynn.
        p.   cm.
    Includes bibliographical references and index.
    ISBN 0-201-58221-X
    1. Mathematica (Computer program) 2. Mathematics--Data processing.   I. Glynn, Jerry.   II. Title.
    QA76.95.G72   1992
    510'.285'536--dc20   91-34568
                                              CIP

Typeset in Palatino and Courier 12pt by the authors, using the *Mathematica* NeXT Front End, designed and written by Theodore W. Gray. Typeset on a Compugraphic 9600 at Wadley Graphix, Champaign, Illinois. Cover color separations done on a Scitex prepress system and output on a Dolev imagesetter at Input/Output, Bloomington, Illinois. Cover design by Andre Kuzniarek.

Reprinted with corrections September, 1992.

2 3 4 5 6 7 8 9 10 - DO - 95949392

Preface

This book is both a tutorial and a reference book. To use it as a tutorial, start at the beginning and read the chapters in order. You will get a good idea of what *Mathematica* does, and will find things explained in a sensible order. To use it as a reference, scan the table of contents to find the question you want answered.

Although this book will get you started using *Mathematica*, it is not a complete reference work. You can't use *Mathematica* effectively without a copy of *Mathematica, a System for Doing Mathematics by Computer*, second edition, by S. Wolfram (see the references section for more information).

We are indebted to several people for help with the book.

Scott May of Wolfram Research suggested the chapter "Why didn't it work when I tried to load a package?", based on the hundreds of people who have had this problem and called him to get it solved. He also suggested the discussion of plotting 3D points as a surface in "How do I plot a list of points?".

Stephen Wolfram made many helpful comments, and suggested the plug for **Trace** in "How do I program in *Mathematica*?".

The following people read manuscripts, and made helpful comments: Henry Edwards, Eva Gray, John Gray, Jerry Keiper, Doug Stein, and Dave Withoff.

David Eisenman edited the entire book, and made it better.

Allan Wylde from Addison-Wesley first proposed that we write the book. We wish him the best of luck with his new publishing endeavors. Peter Gordon, who took over responsibility for the book at Addison-Wesley, encouraged us to increase the book's scope (and quality). Helen Goldstein, Nev Hanke, and several anonymous copyeditors helped tremendously.

Table of Contents

Part Eleven: Notebooks

Part Twelve: Statistics and Data Analysis

Part Thirteen: Programming

Chapter 1
What computer should I use?

This chapter is not about what kind of computer you *could* use to run *Mathematica*. It is about what kind of computer you *should* use. If you plan to buy a computer to run *Mathematica*, you can use this chapter as a buying guide. If you're not planning to buy a computer soon, you can use this chapter as a guide to what kind of computer to borrow, use in a lab, rent, or use as a criterion for choosing friends.

There are four computer worlds: Macintosh, NeXT, MS-DOS, and UNIX. These worlds are very different from each other and do not communicate with each other (except for slight kibitzing between the NeXT and UNIX worlds). When you buy a computer, you are not just buying a computer; you are buying into one of these worlds.

Understand that there are real differences between these worlds. If you buy a Macintosh, you will pay more than you want to. If you buy an MS-DOS computer, you will be limited in the quality of application software you can buy. If you buy a NeXT, you will not be able to find many people around you to help if you have problems. If you buy a UNIX computer, you will have to learn a lot of technical details or employ someone who knows these details.

To make an analogy, an MS-DOS computer is like a 1973 Dodge. A bit creaky, not very comfortable, but as the used car ads say, it runs good. A NeXT computer is like a great deal on a brand new Lamborghini: fast, slick, but hard to get serviced. A UNIX computer is like a kit car: You had better be pretty committed before buying one. A Macintosh is like a

Toyota Camry: good, solid quality, but a little more expensive than it should be.

For many people, the only computer that makes sense is the Macintosh. NeXT and UNIX computers do not have the range of application software (spreadsheets, wordprocessors, desktop publishing software, etc.) that most people need. MS-DOS computers have little software that is not either hard to use or poorly designed. Microsoft Windows is ugly, and too slow except on the fastest 80386- and 80486-based computers, which cost as much as Macintoshes. (The reader may suspect a slight bias in the treatment of MS-DOS computers by at least one of the authors. The reader, in this case, would be correct.)

The Macintosh II*si* is a good choice for many people. The II*lc* is relatively inexpensive and can be upgraded to run *Mathematica* satisfactorily, but be warned that it is not able to use the virtual memory features of System 7 and is therefore ultimately limited (for more information about virtual memory, see Chapter 2, "How do I make my computer work best with *Mathematica*?"). The Macintosh Plus, Classic, and SE are poor choices because they can hold at most 4MB of memory, which is not enough to run *Mathematica* well. The old Macintosh Portable and the new PowerBook 100 are OK, but suffer from the same restrictions as the II*lc*.

The SE-30, Classic II, PowerBook 140, and PowerBook 170 are all good choices. The Classic II is a particularly inexpensive model that supports virtual memory and can run *Mathematica* well. On the high end, the II*fx* and Quadra series are good choices, although they are expensive. Of course, there are always new models of Macintosh coming out, so don't limit yourself to the models discussed here. Any Macintosh capable of supporting virtual memory is OK, and any other Macintosh that supports at least 8MB of RAM is also OK, but not as good as one that supports virtual memory.

The NeXT computer is also a good choice for many people. It is a very exciting computer and is likely to be setting trends for many years to come. The NeXT is a very fast, very powerful computer with a high-quality user interface at a good price (a basic NeXTStation system costs less than a good Macintosh system and runs several times faster). A small number of wordprocessors, spreadsheets, and other software packages are available currently, but not enough to satisfy an aggressive user. More software is likely to be available in the future, and that software is likely to be of a quality comparable to Macintosh software.

UNIX computers are usually a good choice only for computer-oriented people. They are difficult to maintain, requiring extensive familiarity with the UNIX operating system. Sun Microsystems computers come closest to being "end user" computers but are still rather difficult to set up and use. On the other hand, it is possible to buy an incredible amount of raw computer power for very little money in the UNIX market. UNIX computers are usually best used as "compute servers" in departmental or lab settings. If you don't know what that means, you don't want one.

Versions of *Mathematica* are available for almost any computer capable of running it, so that is usually not a factor in choosing your computer. (Be sure to check availability before buying, of course.)

Chapter 2
How do I make my computer work best with *Mathematica*?

Mathematica is a very big program. It is by far the biggest program most people ever run on their computers. Because of this, you may encounter problems with *Mathematica* that are not likely to occur with other programs.

To run *Mathematica*, you must have enough memory and enough disk space. Otherwise, *Mathematica* will not run at all, or it will run very slowly or crash frequently. How much memory is enough? That depends on the brand of computer you are using.

If your computer does not have enough memory or disk space, you will need to upgrade it before using *Mathematica*. As a general rule, it is not a good idea to buy either memory or hard disks from the manufacturer of your computer. You can get both *much* cheaper from specialists who advertise in the backs of computer magazines. (Note that it is usually not necessary to worry about quality. Both memory chips and hard disks are manufactured by only a small number of large companies, all of whom are quite reputable. Small dealers sell exactly the same chips and disks as anyone else; they just have a much lower markup. Most offer a one-year warranty, and in any case the chance of a memory chip or hard disk failing is relatively small: They are pretested and reliable.)

Macintosh

The absolute minimum is 4MB of memory and about 5MB of disk space. If you have only 4MB of memory, you can load *Mathematica* and you can do a few simple calculations, but you can't, for example, do any definite integrals. This is not a practical configuration. In addition, you can't use MultiFinder together with *Mathematica* with only 4MB of memory.

If you have 5MB of memory, you can do quite a bit more. If you have 8MB (the minimum recommended amount) you can do a lot, even with Multi-Finder running.

If you have installed Macintosh System 7, things are a little different. System 7 includes a feature, called virtual memory, that allows you to use space on your hard disk as if it were additional main memory (RAM). Since hard disk space is a lot cheaper than RAM, this allows you to expand your memory cheaply. For example, if you have an 80MB hard disk, you could allot 20MB on the disk for virtual memory. Even if your computer has only a few megabytes of memory, it will act as if it had 20MB of memory.

If you have a Macintosh II, II*cx*, II*ci*, II*si*, II*fx*, SE-30, Classic II, PowerBook 140, PowerBook 170, or Quadra, or any other Macintosh with a 68020, 68030, or 68040 main processor, you can use virtual memory. (Some Macintosh II models require a relatively inexpensive PMMU chip upgrade before they can use virtual memory.) It is reasonable to have as little as 4MB of actual main memory with 8 or more megabytes of virtual memory. It is not at all unreasonable to give *Mathematica* 20 or 30MB of virtual memory in some cases.

Your Macintosh user's manual and the System 7 user's manual explain how to change the amount of virtual memory and the amount allotted to *Mathematica*.

If you have a Macintosh Plus, SE, Classic, LC, PowerBook 100, or any other Mac with a 68000 main processor, you can't use the virtual memory features in System 7. Since System 7 includes only MultiFinder (not Finder), this means that you *cannot* run *Mathematica* and System 7 at all on a machine with less than 8MB that does not support virtual memory. It *is* reasonable to run *Mathematica* and System 7 with 8MB.

NeXT

Special Note! *Mathematica* is *not* compatible with NeXT operating system version 2.0. To run *Mathematica*, you *must* upgrade your NeXT to system 2.1. This upgrade is available free or for a small fee from NeXT or your local NeXT reseller.

Any NeXT computer is able to run *Mathematica*, but the smallest configurations run too slowly. Because NeXT computers use virtual memory, the amount of main memory (RAM) does not affect what you *can* do, only how fast it works. A NeXT with the minimum configuration of 8MB will run *Mathematica*, but too slowly. It is *not* recommended to run *Mathematica* with only 8MB. A NeXTStation or NeXTCube with 14MB or a NeXTStation Color with 20MB is reasonable. A NeXTDimension requires at least 16MB on the main board and 16MB on the display board to give acceptable performance. (If you want to have a lot of windows open at the same time, you need more memory on the display board: 32MB seems to be enough for most people.)

NeXTStation and NeXTCube memory is the same as Macintosh memory: Any 80ns or 100ns Macintosh memory modules will work in a NeXT. (Note that Macintosh IIfx memory is different and doesn't work in anything else.) This means you can buy memory inexpensively from Macintosh memory dealers. NeXTStation Color and NeXTDimension display board memory is different and harder to get: You may have to buy it from NeXT.

Because of the way virtual memory works on the NeXT, the more memory you use, the more disk space it takes up. It is, in fact, possible to completely fill up your hard disk just by running a big calculation in *Mathematica*. This can have serious consequences: You will not be able to save files, for example, and it is even possible to get the disk into a situation where it is no longer possible to start up the computer.

If your NeXT has only a 100MB or 200MB hard disk, you need to pay attention to disk space. **Don't start** *Mathematica* **unless at least 20MB of disk space is free.** After running for a few days, rebooting your NeXT will shrink the virtual memory file to its minimal size; this usually frees up some disk space. You might consider deleting things you don't need, or getting a bigger hard disk.

The NeXT has a SCSI bus for connecting external disks. This means that hard disks are more or less interchangeable between Macintosh, NeXT, and most UNIX computers. Disks that work on one usually also work on the other (although the formatting is completely different, so you can't transfer data this way). This means you can buy inexpensive disks from small dealers. Because there are certain potential incompatibilities, be sure to ask for a NeXT-compatible (or UNIX-compatible) disk.

MS-DOS

Mathematica runs only on 80386, 80486, or newer MS-DOS computers. You will need a numeric coprocessor, and a hard disk. A VGA color screen is also strongly recommended.

The "DOS" version of *Mathematica* runs as a command-line program under the DOS shell. It uses virtual memory, so, in theory, the amount of main memory (RAM) you have does not affect what you can do, only how long it takes. As a practical matter, you need at least 4MB of RAM; if you have less, *Mathematica* will run too slowly to be useful. The DOS version will run comfortably with 6MB.

The virtual memory system used with the DOS version automatically allocates a virtual memory swap file when it is started up, and deletes it when the program exits. The swap file grows bigger as you use more memory. You need to have at least 14MB of free disk space before starting *Mathematica*, to allow room for the swap file to grow. If you intend to do any large calculations, allow more disk space. If the swap file grows to fill your whole disk, you will have trouble!

The swap file works most efficiently if it can be allocated in one (or a small number) of contiguous blocks on your disk. Because of this, it is a good idea to run one of the many disk "optimization" utilities from time to time (the relevant option is often called something like "defragment free space"). These utilities shift the contents of the disk to bring all the free space together in one area.

Microsoft Windows

Mathematica runs only on 80386, 80486, or newer MS-DOS computers. You will need a numeric coprocessor, and a hard disk. A VGA color screen is also strongly recommended.

The "Windows" version of *Mathematica* runs under Microsoft Windows 3.0 (or later versions), and includes the Notebook front end. The Windows version requires somewhat more memory than the "DOS" version.

The Windows version uses Windows virtual memory, so, in theory, the amount of main memory (RAM) you have does not affect what you can do, only how long it takes. However, if you have less than about 6MB of RAM, *Mathematica* will run too slowly to be useful. The Windows version will run comfortably with about 16MB.

You need to allow for at least 16MB of disk space for virtual memory. There are two different ways to do this. You can allocate a "permanent" swap file, which cannot grow, or you can use a "temporary" swap file, which grows bigger as you use more memory, and is deleted when you exit Windows.

The permanent swap file is more efficient (faster) than the temporary one. The main disadvantage is that if you want to use more memory than you initially allocated, you have to go through a relatively lengthy process to reallocate a new, larger, permanent swap file. Also, the disk space allotted to the swap file is not available for other uses, even when you are not using Windows. In addition, certain disks have driver software that is not able to support a permanent swap file.

A temporary swap file can be almost as efficient as a permanent one, provided you run a disk optimization program periodically (the relevant option is often called something like "defragment free space"). The main danger of using a temporary swap file is that it may grow to use up all your free disk space, at which point you will have trouble!

Mathematica users are recommended to upgrade to Windows 3.1 when it becomes available.

UNIX

UNIX computers vary immensely in the way they handle memory and disk space. It is difficult to generalize, but 8MB of main memory and 20MB to 30MB of virtual memory is probably the minimum you want. The installation instructions for *Mathematica* on each type of computer will list the minimum requirements. Generally you will need more than these minimums to run *Mathematica* reasonably well: The minimums are minimal, not typical, requirements.

Chapter 3
How do I start *Mathematica*?

How you start *Mathematica* depends on what brand of computer you are using. *Mathematica* versions can be divided into two main types: Notebook front end and raw terminal.

Notebook front end versions include the Macintosh, NeXT, and Microsoft Windows versions. Raw terminal versions include Sun, DEC, Apollo, and other UNIX versions, and the non-Windows MS-DOS version. This book describes both versions, although some chapters apply only to the Notebook versions.

Whichever version you are using, the first step is to install *Mathematica* on your computer. The procedures for doing this vary widely depending on the computer system, so we can't describe much here. Complete installation instructions come with each copy of *Mathematica*.

If you are using someone else's copy of *Mathematica* (for example, in a student lab or other common area), you should talk to the person in charge to find out where *Mathematica* can be found on the computer you are using.

Once you have installed or located your copy of *Mathematica*, you are ready to start it up. On a Macintosh, NeXT, or MS Windows computer, double-click the *Mathematica* program icon. If this sentence sounds the least bit unfamiliar to you, you may want to take a short detour before continuing with this book.

There are certain basic skills, such as clicking on icons, selecting with the mouse, using menus and dialog boxes, and using the Finder (Macintosh), Workspace (NeXT), or Program Manager (MS Windows), that are common to all programs on a given brand of computer. If you are not familiar with these basic ideas, it's a good idea to spend some time playing with simple programs (word processors, paint programs, games, etc.) before starting to use *Mathematica*. That way you don't have to try to learn two things at the same time.

If you are using a raw terminal version of *Mathematica*, you type "math" at your shell prompt to launch it. If this does *not* launch *Mathematica*, there is a problem with the way it has been installed. Fixing it will require the services of an experienced, trained UNIX (or DOS) expert. If you are not an experienced, trained UNIX (or DOS) expert, do not attempt to solve the problem yourself.

Once *Mathematica* has been launched, you should see an empty window (in Notebook versions), or the input prompt In[1]:= (in raw terminal versions). *Mathematica* is now ready to accept your first expression to evaluate. Proceed to the next chapter.

Chapter 4
Can I read the rest of this book without reading this chapter?

No.

This is a short chapter, but if you don't read it you won't understand anything else in the whole book. As long as you promise to read this chapter, we promise not to be long-winded or to tell you anything that isn't essential.

Know your computer! Most people who drive expensive sports cars in crowded parking lots have learned to drive first. Likewise, it's a good idea to spend a few days with your computer before using a program like *Mathematica*. Write a few letters with your word processor. Draw a picture with the mouse. You should be familiar with how to start ("launch") a program; use the mouse (if you have one) to edit text; scroll; and work with windows and menus (if you have them). You should also be comfortable with the other basic operations of your particular brand of computer.

Capitalization! All of *Mathematica*'s built-in names start with a capital letter: `Sin`, `Table`, `Factor`, `Integrate`, `Expand`, `Plot`, `Pi`, `E`, `I`, etc. Some have more have than one capital letter: `NestList`, `ContourPlot`, `ListDensityPlot`, etc. You must type these names exactly as shown, with the exact capitalization shown, or it won't work.

Square brackets! Functions and commands use square brackets, not parentheses: `Sin[x]`, `Factor[x^2-9]`. If you want to get a sensible answer, you can't say `Sin(x)` or `sin[x]` or `sin(x)`. It has to be exactly `Sin[x]`.

Use the Correct Key! After following the instructions in Chapter 3, "How do I start *Mathematica*?", you will be faced with a blank window (or an "input prompt" if you're using a raw terminal version). To enter an expression, just start typing. Try **2+2**. Then use the "action key" to tell *Mathematica* to carry out the evaluation. This key is different on different kinds of computers:

> **Macintosh:** Enter or Shift-Return. (The Enter key is the one at the far right of the keyboard. Shift-Return means press the return key while holding down the shift key.)
>
> **NeXT:** Enter or Shift-Return.
>
> **MS Windows:** Shift-Enter. (Most DOS keyboards have two enter keys, but they both do the same thing.)
>
> **UNIX or DOS raw terminal versions:** Return. (You can type Shift-Return if you like, it works just as well.)

Here is what a typical session with a Notebook version *Mathematica* might look like:

In[1]:=
> **2+2**

Out[1]=
> 4

The statement we typed is in **boldface** and labeled *In[1]*. *Mathematica*'s result is printed in `plain type` and labeled *Out[1]* (all this happens automatically). In the rest of this book we're not going to show the *In/Out* labels because you rarely need to refer to them.

In a raw terminal version the same session would look like this:

```
In[1]:= 2+2

Out[1]= 4
```

Mathematica automatically typed everything except the 2+2.

Notebooks and Cells! If you are using a Notebook front end version of *Mathematica* (Macintosh, NeXT, or Microsoft Windows), you will see "cell brackets" on the right-hand side of your window as you start entering text and doing evaluations. Do not be alarmed; the cell brackets are quite useful, but you can ignore them at first. Just remember, if you want to start a new input line from scratch, scroll the window (if necessary) so you can see past the bottom of the last piece of text in the window, and click in the area below the last text. You should see a horizontal line across the whole width of the window. This is an indication that you can start typing.

Buy the Book! If you don't have a copy of *Mathematica, a System for Doing Mathematics by Computer*, second edition, by S. Wolfram, stop reading right now and get one. We refer to it as "The *Mathematica* Book" throughout the rest of this book. The *Mathematica* Book describes *all* the functions, commands, constants, and everything else in *Mathematica*. Our book will get you started, but cannot tell you all you'll want to know about how to solve your own problems with *Mathematica*. For that you'll need Wolfram's book. It is available in technical bookstores everywhere, or direct from Addison-Wesley.

Version 2! This book describes features of version 2 of *Mathematica*. Although many of the topics we talk about will work in earlier versions, many of them will not. If you are currently using an older copy of *Mathematica*, it is worthwhile to get it upgraded.

Chapter 5
What do characters like ^, (, [, {, *, %, etc. mean in *Mathematica*?

Some people have trouble getting started with *Mathematica* because of small, distracting, but important details. We don't want this to happen to you, so here are all those details. (Don't look for a plot in this chapter; it's more like a dictionary.)

^ indicates exponentiation: **2^3** is two to the third power.

/ means division; **34/89** is **34** over **89**.

* means multiplication; **34*89** is **34** times **89**.

Space can be used to indicate multiplication: **34 89** is the same as **34*89**. However, spaces often mean nothing at all; **Sin[x]** and **Sin [x]** are the same as **Sin[x]**.

() (Round parentheses) are to be used only to indicate order of evaluation: **(x+3)/x** is the quantity **x+3** divided by **x**. Don't use square brackets or curly brackets to indicate order of evaluation: Only parentheses work.

[] (Square brackets) are used with functions and commands; **Sin[x]** is the sine of **x**. Note that **Sin(x)** does *not* work.

{} (Curly brackets) indicate lists; **{1,3,5,7}** is a list of four numbers.

% represents the result of the last calculation. For example:

```
3*7
```
```
21
```
```
%^2
```
```
441
```

! means factorial; **5!** is **5** factorial.

= means assignment; **a = 5** means set **a** to **5**.

:= also means assignment. See Chapter 38, "How do I program in *Mathematica*?", to find out what the difference is.

== means equality test; **a == 5** returns **True** if **a** is equal to **5**.

!= means not equals; **a != 5** means return **True** if **a** is not equal to **5**. Beware that leaving out the spaces in this example can result in a confusing expression: **a!=5** might mean **a** factorial equals **5**, or **a** not equals **5**. In fact, it is interpreted as **a** not equals **5**, but it's probably best not to rely on this: Just put the spaces in.

<, <=, >, and **>=** mean what you expect.

Chapter 6
What's the difference between numerical and symbolic calculation?

Many people are used to the idea that computers can do arithmetic, but not to the idea that computers can do algebra or calculus. Algebra and calculus are often seen as a higher level than arithmetic; they are not approachable by mere computers. After all, don't computers deal with numbers, not mathematics?

It's true that computers deal with numbers. Only two of them, in fact: 0 and 1. But that's like saying people deal with voltages. Just because our brains process electrical impulses doesn't mean that we can't do algebra.

Unfortunately many people's first exposure is to programs that claim to do algebra or calculus but are just pretending. There are many programs that can do some little bits of mathematics (solve quadratic equations, plot polynomials, manipulate matrices, solve geometry problems). But move beyond the area anticipated by the program's author and things quickly break down.

Mathematica is not like this. It can do algebra, and calculus, and many other kinds of symbolic computations. It is not a trick, it is not a shallow simulation, and it is not a set of preprogrammed examples. It is a deep and sophisticated body of knowledge about how numbers and symbols can be transformed, and it is changing the way mathematics is routinely done by thousands of people.

That said, what does symbolic calculation, the generic name for what *Mathematica* does, really mean?

Many programs (and pocket calculators) can do numerical calculations like this:

27 + 8

35

Mathematica goes beyond this: It can do algebraic calculations, where the answer is not a number:

27 x + 8 x

35 x

With a pocket calculator we can work out the value of the following expression:

(3 + 8)^5

161051

In *Mathematica*, we can use symbolic variable names in place of the numbers **3** and **8**:

(a + b)^5

$(a + b)^5$

We can get the multiplied-out form:

Expand[(a + b)^5]

$a^5 + 5 \, a^4 \, b + 10 \, a^3 \, b^2 + 10 \, a^2 \, b^3 + 5 \, a \, b^4 + b^5$

We can integrate the expression with respect to **a**:

Integrate[(a + b)^5, a]

$\dfrac{a^6}{6} + a^5 \, b + \dfrac{5 \, a^4 \, b^2}{2} + \dfrac{10 \, a^3 \, b^3}{3} + \dfrac{5 \, a^2 \, b^4}{2} + a \, b^5$

Symbolic calculation does not just mean algebra or calculus. For example, *Mathematica* can compute all the permutations of a list of names:

```
Permutations[{Joyce, Eva, Doug, Fernando}]
```

```
{{Joyce, Eva, Doug, Fernando}, {Joyce, Eva, Fernando, Doug},
 {Joyce, Doug, Eva, Fernando}, {Joyce, Doug, Fernando, Eva},
 {Joyce, Fernando, Eva, Doug}, {Joyce, Fernando, Doug, Eva},
 {Eva, Joyce, Doug, Fernando}, {Eva, Joyce, Fernando, Doug},
 {Eva, Doug, Joyce, Fernando}, {Eva, Doug, Fernando, Joyce},
 {Eva, Fernando, Joyce, Doug}, {Eva, Fernando, Doug, Joyce},
 {Doug, Joyce, Eva, Fernando}, {Doug, Joyce, Fernando, Eva},
 {Doug, Eva, Joyce, Fernando}, {Doug, Eva, Fernando, Joyce},
 {Doug, Fernando, Joyce, Eva}, {Doug, Fernando, Eva, Joyce},
 {Fernando, Joyce, Eva, Doug}, {Fernando, Joyce, Doug, Eva},
 {Fernando, Eva, Joyce, Doug}, {Fernando, Eva, Doug, Joyce},
 {Fernando, Doug, Joyce, Eva}, {Fernando, Doug, Eva, Joyce}}
```

Symbolic calculation also applies to expressions involving only numbers. For example, in *Mathematica* we can do calculations involving fractions and get back exact answers:

```
1/3 + 2/5
```

$$\frac{11}{15}$$

We can compute numbers that are larger than most pocket calculators could handle:

```
200!
```

```
78865786736479050355236321393218506229513597768\
  71732632947425332443594499634033429203042840 1\
  19846239041772121389196388302576427902426371 0\
  50619266249528299311134628572707633172373969 8\
  89439224456214516642402540332918641312274282 9\
  48532775242424075739032403212574055795686602 2\
  60319041703240623517008587961789222227896237 0\
  38973747200000000000000000000000000000000000 0\
  0000000000000
```

The \ at the end of each line lets us know that the number continues on the next line.

A general principle in *Mathematica* is that it does not make approximations unless asked to. If we ask a pocket calculator for the square root of 12, it has little choice but to give us a numerical approximation accurate to a few decimal places. If we ask *Mathematica*, it has the option of returning a symbolic result instead:

```
Sqrt[12]
```

    2 Sqrt[3]

Mathematica has rearranged the expression somewhat but has left it with a square root, since there is no better way to represent the answer without making an approximation. If we want a numerical approximation, we can use the **N** function:

```
N[Sqrt[12]]
```

    3.4641

Throughout the rest of this book you will learn about *Mathematica*'s symbolic, numerical, graphical, and programming capabilities.

Chapter 7
How do I make a pretty picture?

You should make a pretty picture with *Mathematica*, preferably on your first day. Let's start with a plain picture and turn it into a pretty one. You should try these plots on your own copy of *Mathematica* to get a feel for how it works. Type exactly what you see here, and you should get the same pictures.

We'll start with a plain picture:

```
Plot[Sin[x], {x, -Pi, Pi}];
```

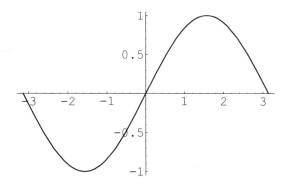

Don't worry about all the brackets; all you need to know is that this is a plot of *sin x* from -π to π.

Let's put in some more trig functions:

```
Plot[Sin[Tan[x]], {x, -Pi, Pi}];
```

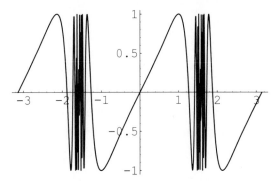

That's more like it. How about using more of the same trig functions:

```
Plot[Sin[Tan[x]-Tan[Sin[x]]], {x, -Pi, Pi}];
```

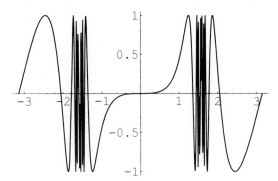

Reshuffling a bit:

```
Plot[Tan[Sin[x]]-Sin[Tan[x]], {x, -Pi, Pi}];
```

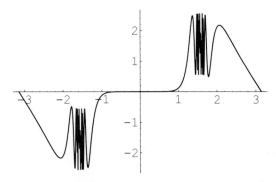

Dividing by **x^7**:

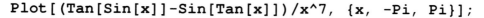

```
Plot[(Tan[Sin[x]]-Sin[Tan[x]])/x^7, {x, -Pi, Pi}];
```

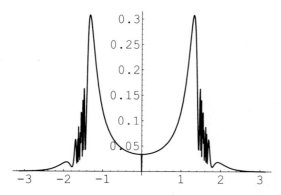

Finally, a pretty picture. (This plot was originally suggested by Ian Mc-Gee of the University of Waterloo.)

Try your own variations! Just remember two things: Use square brackets, and start all function names with capital letters, just as we did in these examples.

Now that we've seen that a pretty picture is not made in one try, we'll show you ten pretty pictures, each the result of lots of experiment, which you won't see. Even if you don't know anything about *Mathematica*, you can take these examples and change them in different ways. You will get lots of pictures, some of them even prettier than the ones here.

Watch out, though. The 3D plots here all take quite a while to evaluate and use quite a lot of memory. Sadly, that is usually the case with pretty 3D pictures. If you have a small computer (e.g., less than 8MB of memory), you might want to stick to the 2D examples.

```
Plot3D[Sin[x + Sin[y]], {x, 0, 4Pi}, {y, 0, 4Pi},
    PlotPoints -> 30];
```

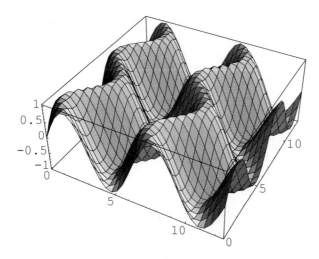

See the middle graphic on the front cover for a color version.

```
ParametricPlot3D[
    {r Cos[t],r Sin[t],0.3+r^2 Sin[4 t+Sin[3 Pi r]]},
    {r, 0, 3}, {t, 0, 2Pi},
    PlotPoints -> {40, 80},
    BoxRatios -> {1, 1, 0.3}
];
```

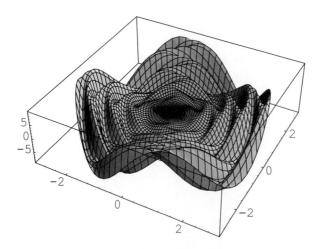

See Figure 7 on the back cover for a color version.

ParametricPlot[{Cos[3 t], Sin[5 t]}, {t, 0, 2Pi}];

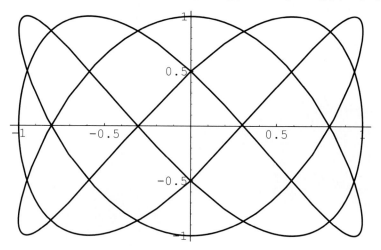

ParametricPlot[{Sin[7 t] Cos[t], Sin[5 t] Sin[t]},
{t, 0, 2Pi}, AspectRatio -> Automatic];

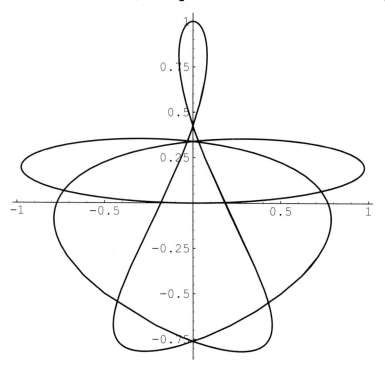

```
ListPlot3D[Table[Mod[i, j], {i, 1, 20}, {j, 1, 20}],
    ViewPoint->{-1.039, 3.189, 0.447}];
```

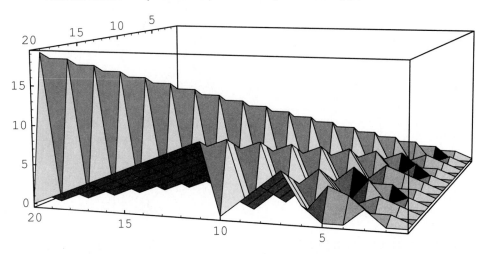

See Figure 8 on the back cover for a color version.

```
Plot[{Sin[x], Sin[Sin[x]]}, {x, -Pi, Pi}];
```

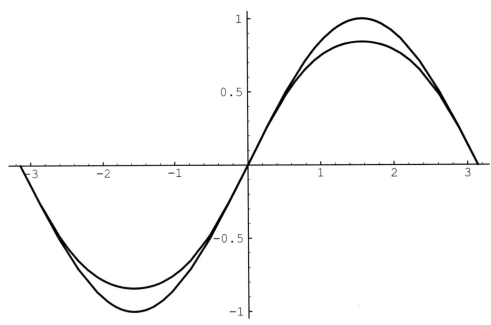

```
DensityPlot[Abs[Gamma[x+y I]],{x, -5, 4},{y, -2, 2},
   PlotPoints -> {100, 50},
   Mesh -> False,
   PlotRange -> {0, 4},
   AspectRatio -> Automatic];
```

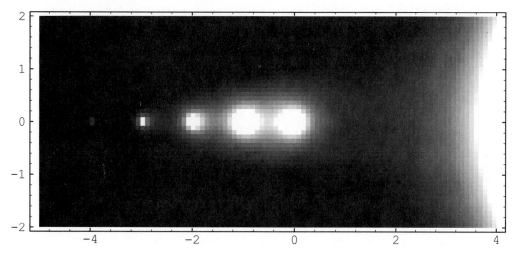

```
Plot[Evaluate[Table[ChebyshevT[n, x], {n, 2, 40}]],
   {x, -1, 1},
   PlotRange -> {-1, 1},
   AspectRatio -> Automatic];
```

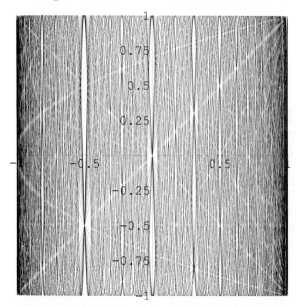

```
ParametricPlot3D[{t (5 + Cos[150 t]) Cos[15 t],
            t (5 + Cos[150 t]) Sin[15 t],
            5 t},
    {t, 0, 2Pi},
    ViewPoint->{0.681, -1.048, 3.144},
    PlotPoints -> 2000];
```

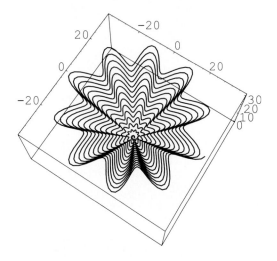

```
ContourPlot[Sin[x / y], {x, -2, 2}, {y, -2, 2},
    PlotPoints -> 30];
```

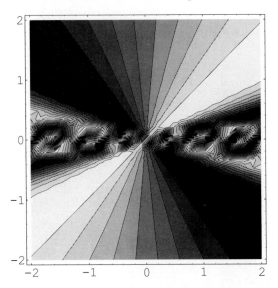

This plot forms the background of the front and back covers of this book.

Chapter 8
How do I ask *Mathematica* for help?

There are several ways to get information about *Mathematica* functions, commands, constants, and options. The ultimate source is always The *Mathematica* Book. Often you can get the information you need more quickly using the help features built into the *Mathematica* kernel.

Likewise, there are several ways to get information about the Notebook front end. In this case the ultimate source is the user's manual that comes with each copy of *Mathematica*. (Since versions of the Notebook front end are somewhat different on different brands of computers, there is no single source.) As with kernel information, you can often get the information you need using built-in help features.

To ask for information about any built-in *Mathematica* symbol (function, command, constant, etc.), use the **?** operator. For example:

```
?Plot

Plot[f, {x, xmin, xmax}] generates a plot of f as a
    function of x from xmin to xmax. Plot[{f1, f2,
    ...}, {x, xmin, xmax}] plots several functions
    fi.
```

Note that the brief description given by **?** does not always include all the forms and variations possible for a given command. It includes only the most common ones. As always, The *Mathematica* Book is the only complete reference.

If you want more information, use **??**:

??Plot

```
Plot[f, {x, xmin, xmax}] generates a plot of f as a
    function of x from xmin to xmax. Plot[{f1, f2,
    ...}, {x, xmin, xmax}] plots several functions
    fi.
```

```
Attributes[Plot] = {HoldAll, Protected}
```

```
Options[Plot] =
  {AspectRatio -> GoldenRatio^(-1),
   Axes -> Automatic, AxesLabel -> None,
   AxesOrigin -> Automatic,
   AxesStyle -> Automatic,
   Background -> Automatic,
   ColorOutput -> Automatic, Compiled -> True,
   DefaultColor -> Automatic, Epilog -> {},
   Frame -> False, FrameLabel -> None,
   FrameStyle -> Automatic,
   FrameTicks -> Automatic, GridLines -> None,
   MaxBend -> 10., PlotDivision -> 20.,
   PlotLabel -> None, PlotPoints -> 25,
   PlotRange -> Automatic,
   PlotRegion -> Automatic,
   PlotStyle -> Automatic, Prolog -> {},
   RotateLabel -> True, Ticks -> Automatic,
   DefaultFont :> $DefaultFont,
   DisplayFunction :> $DisplayFunction}
```

In addition to the command description, **??** also gives the attributes of the function and the default values of all the options that the command accepts. (Don't worry about all the elements in the options list; it is giving more details than most people want to know).

To find out more about one of the options, use **?** again. For example:

?PlotDivision

```
PlotDivision is an option for Plot which specifies
    the maximum amount of subdivision to be used in
    attempting to generate a smooth curve.
```

Notebook versions of *Mathematica* include a shortcut for getting a typical argument list for a function. To use the feature, first type a command name, such as:

Plot

With the text cursor still positioned just after the "**t**", press Command-i (on the Macintosh) or Command-Shift-I (on the NeXT). You will get this:

Plot[f, {x, xmin, xmax}]

The arguments are taken from the first line of the message that **?** gives for the function.

If you don't know the name of the function you are looking for, you can sometimes find it by trying out likely candidates with **?**. For example, if you are looking for Bessel's functions, you might try:

?Bessel

```
Information::notfound1: Symbol Bessel not found.
BesselI BesselJ BesselK BesselY
```

This means that the symbol **Bessel** itself was not found, but the similar symbols **BesselI**, **BesselJ**, **BesselK**, and **BesselY** were. Now you can ask for more specific information about these:

?BesselI

```
BesselI[n, z] gives the modified Bessel function of
    the first kind I(n, z).
```

?BesselJ

```
BesselJ[n, z] gives the Bessel function of the
    first kind J(n, z).
```

?BesselK

```
BesselK[n, z] gives the modified Bessel function of
    the second kind K(n, z).
```

```
?BesselY
```

```
BesselY[n, z] gives the Bessel function of the
    second kind Y(n, z).
```

You can also use the wildcard character "*" (which stands for zero or more arbitrary characters) to find out the names of whole sets of symbols:

```
?*Plot*
```

```
ContourPlot          ParametricPlot3D  PlotPoints
DensityPlot          Plot              PlotRange
ListContourPlot      PlotColor         PlotRegion
ListDensityPlot      PlotDivision      PlotStyle
ListPlot             PlotJoined        Plot3D
ListPlot3D           PlotLabel         Plot3Matrix
ParametricPlot
```

If you are using a Notebook front end version of *Mathematica*, you can use several built-in help features to learn about the front end. Hold down the Command key and type the / key. (If this seems odd, notice that / is just below ? on the same key, so you can think of it as Command-?, except that you don't have to hold down the shift key.)

The mouse pointer will turn into a ? image, indicating that you are now in "help mode". You can now get help about several different kinds of things.

> To find out about any menu command, choose it while in help mode.

> To find out about a feature on the screen, like a scroll bar, window title, etc., click on it while in help mode.

In addition, each dialog box (panel, for NeXT users) has a Help button that can be used to get an explanation of the buttons in it.

Chapter 9
How do I define constants and functions?

In this chapter we're going to define simple functions and constants. Chapter 38, "How do I program in *Mathematica*?", and Chapter 40, "How do I use patterns?", describe how to define more complicated functions.

To define a constant, use a single equals sign:

```
a = 5
5
```

Once defined, you can use the constant anywhere you want:

```
a + 7
12

a^2
25
```

When defining a function, there are only two important things to remember:

- Use an underscore character after each argument name on the left-hand side (but not on the right-hand side).

- Use a := in the middle.

(The reasons for these rules are explained in Chapter 38, "How do I program in *Mathematica*?", and Chapter 40, "How do I use patterns?".)

Here is an example:

```
f[x_] := x^2
```

This function can be applied to many different kinds of arguments. We can use it on a simple number:

```
f[5]
```

```
25
```

We can use it on an expression that evaluates to a number:

```
f[100!]
```

```
87097824890894800794165901619444858655697206439408401342159325362431\
    3799963465833258779670963327549206446903807622196074763642894114311\
    5920190573960677507881394607489905331729758013432992987184764607311\
    7588943431348338296680151515628085416269176619573749317345360351911\
    594496000000000000000000000000000000000000000000000000000000
```

We can use it on a symbolic expression:

```
f[a+b]
```

$(a + b)^2$

Note that there is no problem with variable name conflicts:

```
f[1+x]
```

$(1 + x)^2$

```
f[f[1+x]]
```

$(1 + x)^4$

We can plot the function:

```
Plot[f[x], {x, -2, 2}];
```

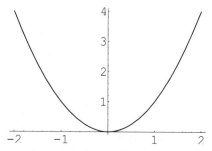

We can take the derivative of the function:

```
D[f[x], x]
2 x
```

In other words, we can use the function in all the same ways that we can use built-in functions.

■ Worked Example

When working a mathematical problem, it is often helpful to define some intermediate quantities. For example, we might want to define the volume of a cylinder as π times the radius squared times the height. We could define such a function like this:

```
volume[radius_, height_] := Pi radius^2 height
```

We can use the function:

```
volume[3, 5]
45 Pi
```

Since we can use symbolic values in the arguments, we can, for example, use units in the arguments:

```
volume[20 Yards, 12 Yards]
4800 Pi Yards^3
```

This is often nice, but seldom thought of.

Chapter 10
How do I load a package?

Many commands are built into *Mathematica*, but many more are defined in "packages". Packages are files that contain definitions of *Mathematica* functions. To use a package, you need to "load" it into *Mathematica*.

To load a package, you need to know its name and the directory (folder) in which it is located. All the packages that come with *Mathematica* are in several subdirectories inside a directory called `Packages`. For example, the package `FilledPlot.m` is inside the directory `Graphics`, inside of `Packages`.

To load `FilledPlot.m`, you can evaluate the following command:

<<Graphics `FilledPlot`

The two single quotes used here are "back quotes" usually found on the same key with ~. They are *not* the single quotes found on the double-quote key. The back-quote character is used to separate the package name from the directory name, and at the end in place of `.m`. The reasons for this are somewhat complex and are explained in detail in The *Mathematica* Book.

In this example, it was not necessary to include the directory `Packages` in the command, because it is one of the directories that *Mathematica* automatically looks in (it is on the directory search path). Which directories are on this list depends on the version of *Mathematica* you are using and how it has been installed. With few exceptions, the `Packages` directory will be on the list. (If you write your own packages and want to load them in, you should read the appropriate sections in The *Mathematica* Book to learn about how to load packages in directories that are not on the list, or how to change the list itself.)

The **<<** command always loads the named package. A more reliable command to use is **Needs**. It loads the specified package only if it has not already been loaded in the same session (loading the same package twice may cause problems). Here is an example:

```
Needs["Graphics`FilledPlot`"]
```

Note that you have to enclose the file name in double quotes.

Don't use any commands defined in a package before you load the package. Doing so will cause problems, as described in Chapter 11, "Why didn't it work when I tried to load a package?".

Chapter 11
Why didn't it work when I tried to load a package?

Suppose you want to plot the area between two curves. Let's pretend you've read Chapter 26, "How do I show the area between curves?", so you know to use the **FilledPlot** command. You might try this example:

FilledPlot[{x^2, Sin[x]}, {x, -5, 5}]

```
FilledPlot[{x , Sin[x]}, {x, -5, 5}]
           2
```

Having this input repeated back to you is not what you wanted!

The problem is that **FilledPlot** is not a built-in function: It doesn't work until you load the package FilledPlot.m. So you reread the chapter and find out that you need to type in and execute the following expression:

Needs["Graphics`FilledPlot`"]

```
FilledPlot::shdw:
    Warning: Symbol FilledPlot
      appears in multiple contexts
    {Graphics`FilledPlot`, Global`}
    ; definitions in context Graphics`FilledPlot`
      may shadow other definitions.
```

Confused by this unexpected message, you ignore it and just try your command again:

FilledPlot[{x^2, Sin[x]}, {x, -5, 5}]

```
FilledPlot[{x , Sin[x]}, {x, -5, 5}]
           2
```

Loading the package seems to have had no effect! The command still doesn't work. Looking more closely at the message, you realize that this "shadow other definitions" may indicate a problem.

Here is what has happened. By using **FilledPlot** *before* loading the package, you made *Mathematica* create an instance of the symbol **FilledPlot** (sort of an empty definition). This definition was entered in the **Global** context. When you loaded FilledPlot.m, you created a new definition for **FilledPlot**, this time in a special context called **Graphics`FilledPlot`**. Unfortunately, when *Mathematica* is looking for a definition, it starts in the **Global** context and looks in other contexts only if it doesn't find a definition there. By using the function once before loading the package, you unwittingly gave it a definition to find in **Global**.

Fortunately, we can escape this mess easily. Evaluate the following command:

Remove[FilledPlot]

This removes the (empty) definition from the **Global** context, allowing the real definition to be seen. Now you can make plots:

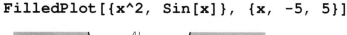

FilledPlot[{x^2, Sin[x]}, {x, -5, 5}]

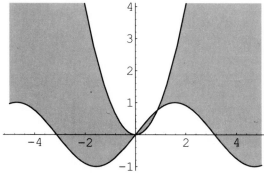

-Graphics-

As a general rule, any time you see a message about "shadowing" when you load a file, it's something to worry about. Using **Remove** on the function(s) named in the message(s) will usually get you out of trouble.

Chapter 12
Can I explore mathematics with *Mathematica*?

Yes.

In earlier times the telescope allowed people to see farther and the microscope closer. *Mathematica* is a tool for modern times. It allows us to see farther and closer into mathematics and to see ideas that are new to us and, once in a while, new to the world.

What does this fluff mean? Let's go through an example of how we can explore a little area of mathematics in an interesting way with *Mathematica*. You don't need to understand the details of the *Mathematica* commands we use here; we'll explain them later. While you read the rest of this book, keep in mind the exploratory mindset of this chapter. We think this is how *Mathematica* should be used.

We asked a number of people if **x^4+64** can be factored without complex numbers. Most said no. Let's see what *Mathematica* says:

> **Factor[x^4+64]**
>
> $(8 - 4 x + x^2) (8 + 4 x + x^2)$

A big surprise for many of us!

How do we follow up on this opportunity? Let's try a few more expressions of this general form and see if they factor:

Factor[x^4+16]

$16 + x^4$

Factor[x^4+36]

$36 + x^4$

Factor[x^4+81]

$81 + x^4$

Factor[x^4+256]

$256 + x^4$

Apparently, many such expressions can't be factored. Typing in examples is going to be a laborious way of finding winners. We can let *Mathematica* run a few more experiments in a short time:

Table[Factor[x^4+n], {n, 1, 12}]

$\{1 + x^4,\ 2 + x^4,\ 3 + x^4,$
$(2 - 2\,x + x^2)\ (2 + 2\,x + x^2),\ 5 + x^4,\ 6 + x^4,$
$7 + x^4,\ 8 + x^4,\ 9 + x^4,\ 10 + x^4,\ 11 + x^4,$
$12 + x^4\}$

We now know that both **x^4+4** and **x^4+64** factor. More clues are needed:

Table[Factor[x^4+n], {n, 13, 36}]

$\{13 + x^4,\ 14 + x^4,\ 15 + x^4,\ 16 + x^4,\ 17 + x^4,\ 18 + x^4,\ 19 + x^4,$
$20 + x^4,\ 21 + x^4,\ 22 + x^4,\ 23 + x^4,\ 24 + x^4,\ 25 + x^4,\ 26 + x^4,$
$27 + x^4,\ 28 + x^4,\ 29 + x^4,\ 30 + x^4,\ 31 + x^4,\ 32 + x^4,\ 33 + x^4,$
$34 + x^4,\ 35 + x^4,\ 36 + x^4\}$

No luck, so let's try some more:

Table[Factor[x^4+n], {n, 37, 70}]

$\{37 + x^4, 38 + x^4, 39 + x^4, 40 + x^4, 41 + x^4, 42 + x^4, 43 + x^4,$
$44 + x^4, 45 + x^4, 46 + x^4, 47 + x^4, 48 + x^4, 49 + x^4, 50 + x^4,$
$51 + x^4, 52 + x^4, 53 + x^4, 54 + x^4, 55 + x^4, 56 + x^4, 57 + x^4,$
$58 + x^4, 59 + x^4, 60 + x^4, 61 + x^4, 62 + x^4, 63 + x^4,$
$(8 - 4 x + x^2) (8 + 4 x + x^2), 65 + x^4, 66 + x^4, 67 + x^4, 68 + x^4,$
$69 + x^4, 70 + x^4\}$

Table[Factor[x^4+n], {n, 71, 135}]

$\{71 + x^4, 72 + x^4, 73 + x^4, 74 + x^4, 75 + x^4, 76 + x^4, 77 + x^4,$
$78 + x^4, 79 + x^4, 80 + x^4, 81 + x^4, 82 + x^4, 83 + x^4, 84 + x^4,$
$85 + x^4, 86 + x^4, 87 + x^4, 88 + x^4, 89 + x^4, 90 + x^4, 91 + x^4,$
$92 + x^4, 93 + x^4, 94 + x^4, 95 + x^4, 96 + x^4, 97 + x^4, 98 + x^4,$
$99 + x^4, 100 + x^4, 101 + x^4, 102 + x^4, 103 + x^4, 104 + x^4,$
$105 + x^4, 106 + x^4, 107 + x^4, 108 + x^4, 109 + x^4, 110 + x^4,$
$111 + x^4, 112 + x^4, 113 + x^4, 114 + x^4, 115 + x^4, 116 + x^4,$
$117 + x^4, 118 + x^4, 119 + x^4, 120 + x^4, 121 + x^4, 122 + x^4,$
$123 + x^4, 124 + x^4, 125 + x^4, 126 + x^4, 127 + x^4, 128 + x^4,$
$129 + x^4, 130 + x^4, 131 + x^4, 132 + x^4, 133 + x^4, 134 + x^4,$
$135 + x^4\}$

Table[Factor[x^4+n], {n, 136, 200}]

$\{136 + x^4, 137 + x^4, 138 + x^4, 139 + x^4, 140 + x^4, 141 + x^4,$
$142 + x^4, 143 + x^4, 144 + x^4, 145 + x^4, 146 + x^4, 147 + x^4,$
$148 + x^4, 149 + x^4, 150 + x^4, 151 + x^4, 152 + x^4, 153 + x^4,$
$154 + x^4, 155 + x^4, 156 + x^4, 157 + x^4, 158 + x^4, 159 + x^4,$
$160 + x^4, 161 + x^4, 162 + x^4, 163 + x^4, 164 + x^4, 165 + x^4,$
$166 + x^4, 167 + x^4, 168 + x^4, 169 + x^4, 170 + x^4, 171 + x^4,$
$172 + x^4, 173 + x^4, 174 + x^4, 175 + x^4, 176 + x^4, 177 + x^4,$
$178 + x^4, 179 + x^4, 180 + x^4, 181 + x^4, 182 + x^4, 183 + x^4,$
$184 + x^4, 185 + x^4, 186 + x^4, 187 + x^4, 188 + x^4, 189 + x^4,$
$190 + x^4, 191 + x^4, 192 + x^4, 193 + x^4, 194 + x^4, 195 + x^4,$
$196 + x^4, 197 + x^4, 198 + x^4, 199 + x^4, 200 + x^4\}$

Table[Factor[x^4+n], {n, 201, 250}]

$\{201 + x^4, 202 + x^4, 203 + x^4, 204 + x^4, 205 + x^4, 206 + x^4,$
$207 + x^4, 208 + x^4, 209 + x^4, 210 + x^4, 211 + x^4, 212 + x^4,$
$213 + x^4, 214 + x^4, 215 + x^4, 216 + x^4, 217 + x^4, 218 + x^4,$
$219 + x^4, 220 + x^4, 221 + x^4, 222 + x^4, 223 + x^4, 224 + x^4,$
$225 + x^4, 226 + x^4, 227 + x^4, 228 + x^4, 229 + x^4, 230 + x^4,$
$231 + x^4, 232 + x^4, 233 + x^4, 234 + x^4, 235 + x^4, 236 + x^4,$
$237 + x^4, 238 + x^4, 239 + x^4, 240 + x^4, 241 + x^4, 242 + x^4,$
$243 + x^4, 244 + x^4, 245 + x^4, 246 + x^4, 247 + x^4, 248 + x^4,$
$249 + x^4, 250 + x^4\}$

This could take forever.

If we look at the two expressions that factored, maybe we can find some clues. We know that **x^4+4** and **x^4+64** factor. Both **4** and **64** are powers of two (**2^2** and **2^6**). Let's guess that if we increase the exponent by the same amount, **4**, we'll get a good one:

```
Factor[x^4+2^10]
```

$$(32 - 8\ x + x^2)\ (32 + 8\ x + x^2)$$

Now we're in business. The next expression to try is **x^4+2^14**:

```
Factor[x^4+2^14]
```

$$(128 - 16\ x + x^2)\ (128 + 16\ x + x^2)$$

It looks like **2** to any power of the form **2+4n** will make an expression that factors. We can make a list of these expressions:

```
Table[Factor[x^4+2^(2+4n)], {n, 0, 10}]
```

$$\{(2 - 2\ x + x^2)\ (2 + 2\ x + x^2),\ (8 - 4\ x + x^2)\ (8 + 4\ x + x^2),$$
$$(32 - 8\ x + x^2)\ (32 + 8\ x + x^2),\ (128 - 16\ x + x^2)\ (128 + 16\ x + x^2)$$
$$(512 - 32\ x + x^2)\ (512 + 32\ x + x^2),$$
$$(2048 - 64\ x + x^2)\ (2048 + 64\ x + x^2),$$
$$(8192 - 128\ x + x^2)\ (8192 + 128\ x + x^2),$$
$$(32768 - 256\ x + x^2)\ (32768 + 256\ x + x^2),$$
$$(131072 - 512\ x + x^2)\ (131072 + 512\ x + x^2),$$
$$(524288 - 1024\ x + x^2)\ (524288 + 1024\ x + x^2),$$
$$(2097152 - 2048\ x + x^2)\ (2097152 + 2048\ x + x^2)\}$$

Perfect! They all factor. Let's see if *Mathematica* can factor the generalized form:

```
Factor[x^4+2^(2+4n)]
```

$$(2\ 2^{2\ n} - 2\ 2^n\ x + x^2)\ (2\ 2^{2\ n} + 2\ 2^n\ x + x^2)$$

We've learned about an interesting class of factorable polynomials. Are there other expressions of the form **x^4 + p** that factor? What do you think? How would you use *Mathematica* to find out?

Chapter 13
What are lists and what can I do with them?

Lists in *Mathematica* are elements enclosed in curly brackets:

```
{10, 20, 30, 40}
```

{10, 20, 30, 40}

Many built-in *Mathematica* commands use or return lists. Here are a few examples (these commands are described in more detail in other chapters):

```
Table[x^2, {x, 1, 10}]
```

{1, 4, 9, 16, 25, 36, 49, 64, 81, 100}

```
Solve[x^2 - 4 == 0, x]
```

{{x -> 2}, {x -> -2}}

```
Plot[{x, x^2, x^3}, {x, -2, 2}];
```

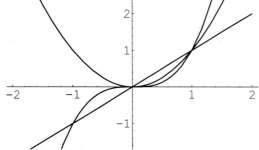

Because lists are used in so many ways in *Mathematica*, it is important to know how to manipulate them. The following examples illustrate the basic things we can do with lists:

We can add a number to each element in a list:

```
5 + {10, 20, 30, 40}
```
{15, 25, 35, 45}

We can multiply each element by a number:

```
5 {10, 20, 30, 40}
```
{50, 100, 150, 200}

We can square each element:

```
{10, 20, 30, 40}^2
```
{100, 400, 900, 1600}

We can join together two lists:

```
Join[{10, 20, 30, 40}, {100, 200, 300, 400}]
```
{10, 20, 30, 40, 100, 200, 300, 400}

We can get an element from a list (the double-square-bracket notation means element of):

```
{10, 20, 30, 40}[[3]]
```
30

We can add two lists element-by-element (note that the lists must have the same number of elements for this to work):

```
{10, 20, 30, 40} + {100, 200, 300, 400}
```
{110, 220, 330, 440}

We can multiply two lists element-by-element:

```
{10, 20, 30, 40} {100, 200, 300, 400}
```
{1000, 4000, 9000, 16000}

Note that this is *not* the dot product of two vectors. Lists as vectors will be explained in Chapter 15, "How do I manipulate vectors and matrices?".

Lists can be rearranged:

Reverse[{10, 20, 30, 40}]

{40, 30, 20, 10}

Sort[{4,2,3,1}]

{1, 2, 3, 4}

Reverse[Sort[{4,2,3,1}]]

{4, 3, 2, 1}

The elements of lists don't have to be numbers:

{x, x^2, x^3, x^4, Sin[x]}

{x, x^2, x^3, x^4, Sin[x]}

If the elements are numbers, we can plot them:

ListPlot[{4, 2, 3, 1, 5, 2, 5, 8, 4, 2, 4, 4, 2}];

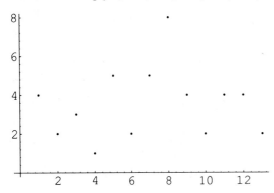

It is possible to have lists of lists, called nested lists. A common case is a list of pairs of numbers:

{{1, 5}, {4, 2}, {1, 3}, {3, 3}, {7,1}, {5,5}, {3,3}, {2,5}}

{{1, 5}, {4, 2}, {1, 3}, {3, 3}}

A list like this can be thought of as a list of x, y points, and **ListPlot** will plot it as such:

```
ListPlot[{{1, 5}, {4, 2}, {1, 3}, {3, 3},
        {7,1}, {5,5}, {3,3}, {2,5}}];
```

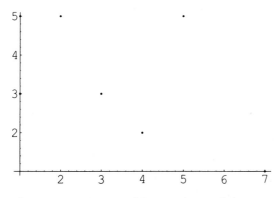

Any arbitrary nesting of lists is possible:

```
{{a, {b, c}, {{d, e, f}}, {g}}}
```
{{a, {b, c}, {{d, e, f}}, {g}}}

Lists are sometimes used in special ways. For example, the **Plot** command has a list as its second argument:

```
Plot[Sin[x], {x, 0, 2Pi}];
```

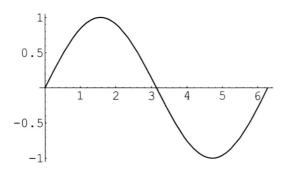

There are many other commands for dealing with lists. We won't go into any more of them; you can look them up in The *Mathematica* Book. They include: **First**, **Last**, **Rest**, **Part**, **Take**, **Drop**, **Prepend**, **Append**, **Insert**, **Delete**, **ReplacePart**, **Union**, **Intersection**, **Complement**, **Transpose**, **RotateLeft**, **RotateRight**, and **Partition**.

▧ Worked Example

In this chapter we had a list of functions for dealing with lists. It wasn't in alphabetical order, but *Mathematica* can sort the list of function names:

```
Sort[{First, Last, Rest, Part, Take, Drop, Prepend,
    Append, Insert, Delete, ReplacePart,
    Union, Intersection, Complement, Transpose,
    RotateLeft, RotateRight, Partition}]
```

```
{Append, Complement, Delete, Drop, First, Insert,
   Intersection, Last, Part, Partition, Prepend,
   ReplacePart, Rest, RotateLeft, RotateRight, Take,
   Transpose, Union}
```

Sort works on all types of expressions, not just numbers. The sorting order is sometimes subtle, but in the case of function names it is alphabetical.

Chapter 14
How do I make a table of values?

One of the most useful applications of *Mathematica*'s list capability is constructing tables of values. Here is a table of squares:

```
Table[n^2, {n, 1, 10}]
```

$$\{1, 4, 9, 16, 25, 36, 49, 64, 81, 100\}$$

- The first argument is the expression that forms each element of the list.
- The second argument is an "iterator specification": In this case it means **n** running from 1 to 10 in steps of 1.

We can change the step size by adding a fourth element to the iterator:

```
Table[n^2, {n, 1, 10, 1/2}]
```

$$\{1, \frac{9}{4}, 4, \frac{25}{4}, 9, \frac{49}{4}, 16, \frac{81}{4}, 25, \frac{121}{4}, 36, \frac{169}{4}, 49,$$
$$\frac{225}{4}, 64, \frac{289}{4}, 81, \frac{361}{4}, 100\}$$

The elements can be symbolic expressions as well:

```
Table[Expand[(1 + x)^n], {n, 1, 5}]
```

$$\{1 + x, \; 1 + 2 x + x^2, \; 1 + 3 x + 3 x^2 + x^3,$$
$$1 + 4 x + 6 x^2 + 4 x^3 + x^4,$$
$$1 + 5 x + 10 x^2 + 10 x^3 + 5 x^4 + x^5\}$$

(**Expand** is explained in Chapter 17, "How do I manipulate polynomials?".)

We can make lists of lists:

```
Table[{n, n^2, n^3, n^4}, {n, 1, 10}]
```

```
{{1, 1, 1, 1}, {2, 4, 8, 16}, {3, 9, 27, 81},
   {4, 16, 64, 256}, {5, 25, 125, 625},
   {6, 36, 216, 1296}, {7, 49, 343, 2401},
   {8, 64, 512, 4096}, {9, 81, 729, 6561},
   {10, 100, 1000, 10000}}
```

In this example we made a list whose elements are also lists.

In the next example we make the same list, but using a second iterator:

```
Table[n^a, {n, 1, 10}, {a, 1, 4}]
```

```
{{1, 1, 1, 1}, {2, 4, 8, 16}, {3, 9, 27, 81},
   {4, 16, 64, 256}, {5, 25, 125, 625},
   {6, 36, 216, 1296}, {7, 49, 343, 2401},
   {8, 64, 512, 4096}, {9, 81, 729, 6561},
   {10, 100, 1000, 10000}}
```

• The first argument is the expression that forms each element of the list.
• The second argument is the "slow" iterator (the one that changes when you go from one inner list to the next).
• The third argument is the "fast" iterator (the one that changes from one element to the next inside each of the inner lists).

It is frequently useful to add **//TableForm** to the end of commands like this one. **TableForm** displays lists, and lists of lists, in a two-dimensional layout:

```
{{a, b}, {c, d}}//TableForm
```

```
a   b
c   d
```

```
Table[n^a, {n, 1, 10}, {a, 1, 4}]//TableForm
```

1	1	1	1
2	4	8	16
3	9	27	81
4	16	64	256
5	25	125	625
6	36	216	1296
7	49	343	2401
8	64	512	4096
9	81	729	6561
10	100	1000	10000

■ Worked Example

Jerry: Three years ago, all the math teachers I knew who were using graphing programs were trading "hard" problems. One of the best was "find the intersections of **x^10** and **2^x**". I quickly found two obvious points of intersection with one plot:

```
Plot[{x^10, 2^x}, {x, -2, 2}];
```

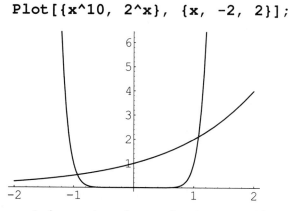

For more information about plotting, see Chapter 22, "How do I plot a function in two dimensions?".

I began to wonder why this was considered a "hard" problem. I decided there must be more to it and went looking for a third point of intersection. I was successful only when I started making tables. Here are the tables that finally cracked the problem:

```
Table[N[{x, x^10, 2^x, x^10 - 2^x}],
     {x, -5, 5}]//TableForm
```

-5.	$9.76562 \ 10^6$	0.03125	$9.76562 \ 10^6$
-4.	$1.04858 \ 10^6$	0.0625	$1.04858 \ 10^6$
-3.	59049.	0.125	59048.9
-2.	1024.	0.25	1023.75
-1.	1.	0.5	0.5
0	0	1.	-1.
1.	1.	2.	-1.
2.	1024.	4.	1020.
3.	59049.	8.	59041.
4.	$1.04858 \ 10^6$	16.	$1.04856 \ 10^6$
5.	$9.76562 \ 10^6$	32.	$9.76559 \ 10^6$

The right-most column is the difference between the two functions. It must change sign every time the functions cross. Looking at the right-most column, we see that there must be one crossing between -1 and 0, and another between 1 and 2. We can make another table to isolate the first crossing:

```
Table[N[{x, x^10, 2^x, x^10 - 2^x}],
     {x, -1, -0.1, 0.1}]//TableForm
```

-1.	1.	0.5	0.5
-0.9	0.348678	0.535887	-0.187208
-0.8	0.107374	0.574349	-0.466975
-0.7	0.0282475	0.615572	-0.587325
-0.6	0.00604662	0.659754	-0.653707
-0.5	0.000976563	0.707107	-0.70613
-0.4	0.000104858	0.757858	-0.757753
-0.3	$5.9049 \ 10^{-6}$	0.812252	-0.812246
-0.2	$1.024 \ 10^{-7}$	0.870551	-0.87055
-0.1	$1. \ 10^{-10}$	0.933033	-0.933033

We could repeat this process to narrow in on the two crossings.

To try to find the third crossing, we can look farther and farther from the origin:

```
Table[N[{x, x^10, 2^x, x^10 - 2^x}],
     {x, 10, 30, 2}]//TableForm
```

10.	$1.\ 10^{10}$	1024.	$1.\ 10^{10}$
12.	$6.19174\ 10^{10}$	4096.	$6.19174\ 10^{10}$
14.	$2.89255\ 10^{11}$	16384.	$2.89255\ 10^{11}$
16.	$1.09951\ 10^{12}$	65536.	$1.09951\ 10^{12}$
18.	$3.57047\ 10^{12}$	262144.	$3.57047\ 10^{12}$
20.	$1.024\ 10^{13}$	$1.04858\ 10^{6}$	$1.024\ 10^{13}$
22.	$2.65599\ 10^{13}$	$4.1943\ 10^{6}$	$2.65599\ 10^{13}$
24.	$6.34034\ 10^{13}$	$1.67772\ 10^{7}$	$6.34034\ 10^{13}$
26.	$1.41167\ 10^{14}$	$6.71089\ 10^{7}$	$1.41167\ 10^{14}$
28.	$2.96197\ 10^{14}$	$2.68435\ 10^{8}$	$2.96196\ 10^{14}$
30.	$5.9049\ 10^{14}$	$1.07374\ 10^{9}$	$5.90489\ 10^{14}$

It looks hopeless: How can the difference ever change sign again when the difference is getting bigger and bigger? Perhaps it already changed sign, and then changed back again within the space between our table entries! But we plod on:

```
Table[N[{x, x^10, 2^x, x^10 - 2^x}],
     {x, 40, 60, 2}]//TableForm
```

40.	$1.04858\ 10^{16}$	$1.09951\ 10^{12}$	$1.04847\ 10^{16}$
42.	$1.70802\ 10^{16}$	$4.39805\ 10^{12}$	$1.70758\ 10^{16}$
44.	$2.71974\ 10^{16}$	$1.75922\ 10^{13}$	$2.71798\ 10^{16}$
46.	$4.24207\ 10^{16}$	$7.03687\ 10^{13}$	$4.23504\ 10^{16}$
48.	$6.49251\ 10^{16}$	$2.81475\ 10^{14}$	$6.46436\ 10^{16}$
50.	$9.76562\ 10^{16}$	$1.1259\ 10^{15}$	$9.65304\ 10^{16}$
52.	$1.44555\ 10^{17}$	$4.5036\ 10^{15}$	$1.40052\ 10^{17}$
54.	$2.10833\ 10^{17}$	$1.80144\ 10^{16}$	$1.92818\ 10^{17}$
56.	$3.03305\ 10^{17}$	$7.20576\ 10^{16}$	$2.31248\ 10^{17}$
58.	$4.30804\ 10^{17}$	$2.8823\ 10^{17}$	$1.42574\ 10^{17}$
60.	$6.04662\ 10^{17}$	$1.15292\ 10^{18}$	$-5.4826\ 10^{17}$

Wow! Suddenly, between 58 and 60, the difference shoots down below zero. That means there must be a crossing point, which we can narrow in on:

```
Table[N[{x, x^10, 2^x, x^10 - 2^x}],
      {x, 58, 59, 0.1}]//TableForm
```

58.	4.30804×10^{17}	2.8823×10^{17}	1.42574×10^{17}
58.1	4.3829×10^{17}	3.08918×10^{17}	1.29372×10^{17}
58.2	4.45892×10^{17}	3.3109×10^{17}	1.14802×10^{17}
58.3	4.53613×10^{17}	3.54853×10^{17}	9.87598×10^{16}
58.4	4.61454×10^{17}	3.80322×10^{17}	8.11318×10^{16}
58.5	4.69417×10^{17}	4.07619×10^{17}	6.17975×10^{16}
58.6	4.77503×10^{17}	4.36876×10^{17}	4.06275×10^{16}
58.7	4.85714×10^{17}	4.68232×10^{17}	1.74828×10^{16}
58.8	4.94053×10^{17}	5.01838×10^{17}	-7.78555×10^{15}
58.9	5.0252×10^{17}	5.37857×10^{17}	-3.53374×10^{16}
59.	5.11117×10^{17}	5.76461×10^{17}	-6.5344×10^{16}

```
Table[N[{x, x^10, 2^x, x^10 - 2^x}],
      {x, 58.7, 58.8, 0.01}]//TableForm
```

58.7	4.85714×10^{17}	4.68232×10^{17}	1.74828×10^{16}
58.71	4.86543×10^{17}	4.71488×10^{17}	1.50541×10^{16}
58.72	4.87372×10^{17}	4.74768×10^{17}	1.2604×10^{16}
58.73	4.88203×10^{17}	4.7807×10^{17}	1.01323×10^{16}
58.74	4.89034×10^{17}	4.81395×10^{17}	7.639×10^{15}
58.75	4.89868×10^{17}	4.84744×10^{17}	5.12381×10^{15}
58.76	4.90702×10^{17}	4.88115×10^{17}	2.58661×10^{15}
58.77	4.91538×10^{17}	4.91511×10^{17}	2.72328×10^{13}
58.78	4.92375×10^{17}	4.94929×10^{17}	-2.55448×10^{15}
58.79	4.93213×10^{17}	4.98372×10^{17}	-5.15868×10^{15}

Now we know the crossing point is between 58.77 and 58.78.

Let's make some plots, first of the two easy crossings again:

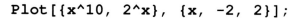

Plot[{x^10, 2^x}, {x, -2, 2}];

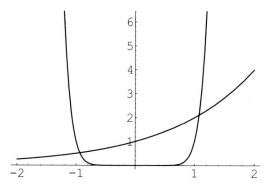

It's pretty clear from this picture that the **x^10** curve is heading up *much* faster than the **2^x** curve. Let's plot farther out:

Plot[{x^10, 2^x}, {x, 0, 20}];

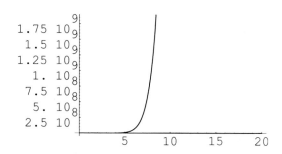

The **x^10** is so huge that the **2^x** is flattened against the *x* axis. Clearly these curves are never, ever going to cross. But we plod (and plot) on:

Plot[{x^10, 2^x}, {x, 0, 60}, PlotRange -> All];

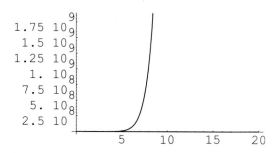

Incredibly, **2^x** does catch up in the end. Now it's the one that is obviously rising *much* faster than **x^10**. Clearly these curves are never, ever going
to cross again.

If we want to find the exact point of intersection, we can use the **FindRoot**
function:

```
FindRoot[x^10 == 2^x, {x, 58}, WorkingPrecision->20]
{x -> 58.7701059379213756}
```

(For more information about **FindRoot**, see The *Mathematica* Book. We're
just using it to show you the exact answer.) Without the tables and plots,
we would not have known what starting value to give **FindRoot**. Without
a good starting point, **FindRoot** will never find the third intersection.

Chapter 15
How do I manipulate vectors and matrices?

Vectors in *Mathematica* are lists:

```
{x, y}
```
{x, y}

Mathematica doesn't distinguish between column vectors and row vectors. A list like the one above can be either, depending on how you choose to use it.

Matrices are lists of lists:

```
{{a, b}, {c, d}}
```
{{a, b}, {c, d}}

To see this in more traditional notation, we can add **//MatrixForm**:

```
{{a, b}, {c, d}}//MatrixForm
```
a   b
c   d

Chapter 13, "What are lists and what can I do with them?", and Chapter 14, "How do I make a table of values?", describe many functions you can use with lists. Most of these functions can be useful when dealing with vectors and matrices as well, since vectors, matrices, and lists are very much the same thing in *Mathematica*.

We can take the dot product of vectors and/or matrices using the "." operator:

```
{{a, b}, {c, d}} . {x, y}
{a x + b y, c x + d y}

{x, y} . {{a, b}, {c, d}}
{a x + c y, b x + d y}
```

In the first case `{x, y}` is acting as a column vector, while in the second case it is acting as a row vector. It can act as both at the same time:

```
{x, y} . {x, y}
```
$$x^2 + y^2$$

The following are some of *Mathematica*'s built-in vector and matrix manipulation functions. All of these functions work on both numerical and symbolic matrices. We'll demonstrate them on simple symbolic matrices so you can see the results:

```
Det[{{a, b}, {c, d}}]
- (b c) + a d

Transpose[{{a, b}, {c, d}}]//MatrixForm
a    c
b    d

Inverse[{{a, b}, {c, d}}]//MatrixForm
```

$$\frac{d}{-(b\ c)\ +\ a\ d} \qquad -\left(\frac{b}{-(b\ c)\ +\ a\ d}\right)$$

$$-\left(\frac{c}{-(b\ c)\ +\ a\ d}\right) \qquad \frac{a}{-(b\ c)\ +\ a\ d}$$

```
IdentityMatrix[3]//MatrixForm
1    0    0
0    1    0
0    0    1
```

```
DiagonalMatrix[{a,b,c}]//MatrixForm
```

```
a   0   0
0   b   0
0   0   c
```

```
Array[a, {3, 3}]//MatrixForm
```

```
a[1, 1]    a[1, 2]    a[1, 3]
a[2, 1]    a[2, 2]    a[2, 3]
a[3, 1]    a[3, 2]    a[3, 3]
```

```
Dimensions[{{a, b, c}, {d, e, f}}]
```

```
{2, 3}
```

```
Eigenvalues[{{a, b}, {c, d}}]
```

$$\left\{\frac{a + d + \text{Sqrt}[a^2 + 4\ b\ c - 2\ a\ d + d^2]}{2},\right.$$

$$\left.\frac{a + d - \text{Sqrt}[a^2 + 4\ b\ c - 2\ a\ d + d^2]}{2}\right\}$$

```
Eigenvectors[{{a, b}, {c, d}}]
```

$$\left\{\left\{\frac{a - d - \text{Sqrt}[a^2 + 4\ b\ c - 2\ a\ d + d^2]}{2\ c}, 1\right\},\right.$$

$$\left.\left\{\frac{a - d + \text{Sqrt}[a^2 + 4\ b\ c - 2\ a\ d + d^2]}{2\ c}, 1\right\}\right\}$$

Symbolic matrices larger than about 3 by 3 often produce eigenvalues and eigenvectors that are *HUGE* expressions, and take a long time to compute and print out.

Eigensystem is a combination of **Eigenvalues** and **Eigenvectors**: it returns a list whose first element is a list of eigenvalues and whose second element is a list of eigenvectors. (If you want both, it is faster to use **Eigensystem** instead of both **Eigenvalues** and **Eigenvectors**.)

```
Eigensystem[{{a, b}, {c, d}}]
```

$$\left\{\left\{\frac{a + d - \mathrm{Sqrt}[a^2 + 4\ b\ c - 2\ a\ d + d^2]}{2},\right.\right.$$

$$\left.\frac{a + d + \mathrm{Sqrt}[a^2 + 4\ b\ c - 2\ a\ d + d^2]}{2}\right\},$$

$$\left\{\left\{\frac{a - d - \mathrm{Sqrt}[a^2 + 4\ b\ c - 2\ a\ d + d^2]}{2\ c},\ 1\right\},\right.$$

$$\left.\left\{\frac{a - d + \mathrm{Sqrt}[a^2 + 4\ b\ c - 2\ a\ d + d^2]}{2\ c},\ 1\right\}\right\}\right\}$$

CharacteristicPolynomial returns a polynomial whose roots are the eigenvalues of the matrix, written in terms of the variable given in its second argument.

```
CharacteristicPolynomial[{{a, b}, {c, d}}, x]
```

$$-(b\ c) + a\ d - a\ x - d\ x + x^2$$

We can demonstrate that this is the case by solving the polynomial:

```
Solve[
CharacteristicPolynomial[{{a, b}, {c, d}}, x]==0, x]
```

$$\left\{\left\{x \rightarrow \frac{a + d + \mathrm{Sqrt}[a^2 + 4\ b\ c - 2\ a\ d + d^2]}{2}\right\},\right.$$

$$\left.\left\{x \rightarrow \frac{a + d - \mathrm{Sqrt}[a^2 + 4\ b\ c - 2\ a\ d + d^2]}{2}\right\}\right\}$$

Many other vector and matrix manipulation functions are available in *Mathematica,* but to use them we have to execute the following command first:

```
Needs["LinearAlgebra`Master`"];
```

(Note that the two single quotes used here are "back quotes" usually found on the same key with ~. They are *not* the single quotes found on the double-quote key.) The command loads in a set of standard packages (included in all copies of *Mathematica* Version 2).

We won't go into any more detail about most of these functions. They are described in the Guide to Standard Packages that comes with each copy of *Mathematica*.

One of the most useful and frequently requested functions defined in these packages is the cross product:

```
Cross[{a, b, c}, {x, y, z}]
{-(c y) + b z, c x - a z, -(b x) + a y}
```

Chapter 16
What's the difference between 2 and 2.?

A general principle in *Mathematica* is that it does not make approximations unless asked to do so. When we apply **Sqrt** to the integer 2, *Mathematica* returns the expression unchanged:

    Sqrt[2]

    Sqrt[2]

There is no better way to write this without making an approximation.

On the other hand, if we apply **Sqrt** to a decimal number like **2.5**, *Mathematica* will compute the square root automatically, because it assumes that **2.5** is already approximate:

    Sqrt[2.5]

    1.58114

Just adding a decimal point to an integer is enough to let *Mathematica* know that we mean an approximate number, not an exact integer:

    Sqrt[2.]

    1.41421

Although it may seem somewhat strange, **2** and **2.** are different: The first is an exact integer, while the second is an approximate decimal number.

We can convert an exact integer into an approximate number using the **N** function:

```
N[2]
```

```
2.
```

Notice that the result has a decimal point in it.

The **N** function can be applied to entire expressions:

```
N[Sqrt[2]]
```

```
1.41421
```

We can use a second argument to **N** to specify the number of decimal places of precision desired:

```
N[Sqrt[2], 40]
```

```
1.414213562373095048801688724209698078857
```

Look what happens when we repeat this command using **2.** instead of **2**:

```
N[Sqrt[2.], 40]
```

```
1.414213562373095
```

This is *Mathematica* being careful: The **2.** is assumed to be an approximate number of, by default, about 18 digits of precision ("machine precision"). Since the starting point of the calculation was accurate to only 18 places, asking for 40 places in the answer was not appropriate. If we want high-precision answers, we have to start either with exact integers (which have infinite precision), or with approximate numbers with enough places of precision:

```
N[Sqrt[2.00000000000000000000000000000000000000],
   40]
```

```
1.414213562373095048801688724209698078857
```

Mathematica automatically propagates the appropriate precision in calculations, so we don't really need the **N** in the example above:

Sqrt[2.000000000000000000000000000000000000000]

1.4142135623730950488016887242096980785 7

Note that precision can be lost in a calculation:

N[10^20 + Sqrt[2], 40]

$1.000000000000000000001414213562373095 0488 \ 10^{20}$

% - 10^20

1.4142135623730950488

(**%** means the last result.) The answer is accurate to only about 20 places, even though we started with 40. *Mathematica* lets us know this by printing only the accurate digits. It is possible to do a calculation which results in *no* accurate digits:

N[10^50 + Sqrt[2], 40] - 10^50

0.

10^50 accurate to 40 decimal places means **10^50 ± 10^10**. Adding 1.414 to this has no effect: it's far smaller than the resolution of the number.

When you use **N** and specify precision to a certain number of places, you will not always get the number of places you ask for. The numbers in the calculation are converted to the number of places requested, but from then on *Mathematica* propagates the precision according to the appropriate rules. By the time the calculation is finished, you may have fewer (or sometimes even more) places than you asked for.

■ Worked Example

Jerry: Adjustments are required, for some of us, as we move further into the computer age. Many of us used to think that 2, or 2.0, or 2.000 were basically the same. Obviously a chemist or engineer making a measurement has seen them as quite different all along. Now the rest of us should follow their lead.

The idea of "losing precision" in a calculation seems reasonable, and once in a while you might be lucky enough to *maintain* the same precision through a calculation. But *increasing* the precision through a calculation seems a bit odd, even magical. How can this be?

Theo: If you add a small number to a large, exact number, you can increase the precision:

```
10^20 + N[Sqrt[2], 20]
```

$$1.0000000000000000000141421356237309504888 \; 10^{20}$$

We got an answer with about 40 digits, even though we started with 20. Of course, you could say that we started with infinite precision (the integer `10^20`) and reduced it to only 40.

Chapter 17
How do I manipulate polynomials?

Factoring and expanding are a good place to start:

    Factor[a^2 + 2 a b + b^2]

$(a + b)^2$

    Expand[(a+b)^5]

$a^5 + 5 a^4 b + 10 a^3 b^2 + 10 a^2 b^3 + 5 a b^4 + b^5$

By default, *Mathematica* factors over the integers, so this example doesn't factor:

    Factor[x^2 + 9]

$9 + x^2$

If we want to allow complex numbers, we can use the following variation:

    Factor[x^2 + 9, GaussianIntegers -> True]

$(-3 I + x) (3 I + x)$.

GaussianIntegers -> True is what's called an option. Don't worry about what **GaussianIntegers** means: it's a somewhat pretentious term for "I want to allow complex numbers (with integer coefficients) in the answer."

Mathematica does not "factor over the radicals":

```
Factor[x^2 - 3]
```

$$-3 + x^2$$

Factoring over the radicals is not factoring in the usual sense of the word; it is more like finding the roots of the expression, which can be done with the **Solve** command:

```
Solve[x^2 - 3 == 0, x]
```

```
{{x -> Sqrt[3]}, {x -> -Sqrt[3]}}
```

This somewhat strange-looking result means that the two roots are the square root of three, and the negative of that. See Chapter 18, "How do I solve equations?", for more information about the **Solve** command and an explanation of its result format.

If you factor a polynomial involving fractions, *Mathematica* puts everything over a common denominator:

```
Factor[x^2 - 4/9]
```

$$\frac{(-2 + 3\ x)\ (2 + 3\ x)}{9}$$

Mathematica can factor expressions involving functions as well as simple variables:

```
Factor[Sin[x]^2 - Cos[x]^2]
```

```
(-Cos[x] + Sin[x]) (Cos[x] + Sin[x])
```

```
Factor[Sin[x]^2 - E^(2x)]
```

$$(-E^x + Sin[x])\ (E^x + Sin[x])$$

There are several commands for carrying out structural rearrangements of expressions. Here are some examples:

Combining terms over a common denominator:

Together[a/b + c/d]

$$\frac{b\ c + a\ d}{b\ d}$$

Splitting fractions apart:

Apart[(b c + a d)/(b d)]

$$\frac{a}{b} + \frac{c}{d}$$

Collecting coefficients of equal powers of the variable specified by the second argument:

Collect[a x + b x + c y + d y, x]

(a + b) x + c y + d y

Simplifying:

Simplify[(x^2 + 2 x y + y^2) / (x + y)]

x + y

Simplify is a very complex command. It tries to find the "simplest" form of the expression. It is often not clear which of several possible forms is the simplest, and different people may consider different forms to be simpler. *Mathematica*'s definition of simplest is having the least number of elements.

Chapter 18
How do I solve equations?

The **Solve** command can be used to solve equations:

```
Solve[x^2 - 2 x == 0, x]
{{x -> 2}, {x -> 0}}
```

• The first argument is the equation to be solved.
• The second argument is the variable for which we're solving.

(In *Mathematica*, **==** means equality. Single **=** means assignment.)

The result is given in the form of a list of replacement rules (**->**). In this case the solution shown is **x** equals **2** or **0**. (The astute reader may notice that the result is actually a list of *lists of* replacement rules. We can ignore this for now and look at the expressions to the right of the arrows.)

If your equation involves other variables, they will be treated as constants:

```
Solve[x^2 - 5 x y + 4 y^2 == 0, x]
{{x -> 4 y}, {x -> y}}
```

You can solve systems of equations involving more than one variable by using lists for both the first and second arguments to **Solve**:

```
Solve[{2 x + 3 y == 7, 3 x - 2 y == 11}, {x, y}]
```
$$\{\{x \to \frac{47}{13}, y \to -(\frac{1}{13})\}\}$$

• The first argument is a list of the equations to be solved.
• The second argument is a list of the variables to be solved for.

The system above had one solution. If there is more than one solution, you will get a list of lists of values:

```
Solve[{x^2 + y^2 == 16, x^2 - 4 == y}, {x, y}]
```
```
{{y -> 3, x -> Sqrt[7]}, {y -> 3, x -> -Sqrt[7]},
    {y -> -4, x -> 0}, {y -> -4, x -> 0}}
```

The first element of the result, `{y -> 3, x -> 7^(1/2)}`, is the first solution, and so on.

Adding the useful command `//TableForm` to such a `Solve` command causes the output to be formatted more readably:

```
Solve[{x^2+y^2 == 16, x^2-4 == y}, {x, y}]//TableForm
```
```
y -> 3       x -> Sqrt[7]
y -> 3       x -> -Sqrt[7]
y -> -4      x -> 0
y -> -4      x -> 0
```

Each row represents one solution. (Notice the double root.)

If there is no solution, an empty list is returned:

```
Solve[{x^2 == 3, x^2 == 4}, x]
```
```
{}
```

`Solve` returns a list of replacement rules because this is a versatile form to have the results in. It shows the results in a fairly clear way, and it can be used to calculate the value of expressions involving the variables.

To explain replacement rules, here are some examples:

```
x^2 /. x -> 5
```
```
25
```

This means replace **x** with **5** in the expression **x^2**. The **/.** operator should be read "replace" and **->** should be read "with". The whole expression is "in **x^2** replace **x** with **5**".

You can use a list of rules to replace more than one variable at a time:

```
x^2 + y^2 /. {x -> 5, y-> 10}
```
```
125
```

When we use a list of lists of replacement rules, we get a list of results:

```
x^2 /. {{x -> 5}, {x -> 6}}
```
```
{25, 36}
```

```
x^2 + y^2 /. {{x -> 5, y-> 10}, {x -> 6, y-> 10}}
```
```
{125, 136}
```

Returning to the first example in this chapter:

```
solution = Solve[x^2 - 2 x == 0, x]
```
```
{{x -> 2}, {x -> 0}}
```

This is a list of lists of replacement rules, and we can use it to replace values in any expression we like. For example, we can check that the answer is correct by substituting the solution into the original expression:

```
x^2 - 2 x /. solution
```
```
{0, 0}
```

The list of two zeros indicates that both solutions give a value of zero when substituted into the original expression.

We can use the **Solve** command directly in the replace expression:

```
x^2 /. Solve[x^2 == 4, x]
```
```
{4, 4}
```

These two **4**'s are the result of substituting the two solutions in the the expression **x^2**.

To get a simple list of the values of the solution, use the following form:

```
x /. Solve[x^2 == 4, x]
```
```
{2, -2}
```

For more information about how lists and replacement rules interact, see
The *Mathematica* Book.

Some equations (for example, some polynomials of fifth degree and
higher) can't be solved in explicit form:

```
Solve[x^6 + x^5 + x^2 + 1 == 0, x]
```

$\{ \text{ToRules}[\text{Roots}[x^2 + x^5 + x^6 == -1, x]] \}$

(Ignore the result; it's confusing.) Using the **N** function you can get a
numerical approximation to the solution:

```
N[Solve[x^6 + x^5 + x^2 + 1 == 0, x]]//TableForm
x -> -1.15408 - 0.613723 I
x -> -1.15408 + 0.613723 I
x -> -0.08275 - 0.795302 I
x -> -0.08275 + 0.795302 I
x -> 0.736832 - 0.610339 I
x -> 0.736832 + 0.610339 I
```

The imaginary constant (square root of -1) is represented by **I**, which is
consistent with *Mathematica*'s rule that all built-in functions, constants, and
variables start with a capital letter.

If you want higher precision, you can add a second argument to the **N**
function, specifying the number of digits to work with:

```
N[Solve[x^6 + x^5 + x^2 + 1 == 0, x], 20]//TableForm
x -> -1.1540824762585313148 - 0.61372296835498784283 I
x -> -1.1540824762585313148 + 0.61372296835498784283 I
x -> -0.08275000929153482285 - 0.79530242822820603419 I
x -> -0.08275000929153482285 + 0.79530242822820603419 I
x -> 0.73683248555006613766 - 0.61033941669740026683 I
x -> 0.73683248555006613766 + 0.61033941669740026683 I
```

Chapter 19
How do I integrate and differentiate?

Two basic commands for doing calculus in *Mathematica* are **Integrate** and **D** (for differentiate). Here is how to integrate a function:

```
Integrate[x^2, x]
```

$$\frac{x^3}{3}$$

- The first argument, **x^2**, is the expression to be integrated.
- The second argument, **x**, is the variable to integrate with respect to.

You can integrate expressions containing more than one variable; the other variables are treated as constants:

```
Integrate[a x^2, x]
```

$$\frac{a\ x^3}{3}$$

```
Integrate[x^2 y^3, x]
```

$$\frac{x^3\ y^3}{3}$$

Differentiation with the **D** command has the same form as integration:

```
D[x^2, x]
```

$$2\ x$$

```
D[a x^2, x]
```

2 a x

```
D[x^2 y^3, x]
```

2 x y³

To do a definite integral, use a list as the second argument. This command gives the integral of **x^2** from **0** to **1**:

```
Integrate[x^2, {x, 0, 1}]
```

$\frac{1}{3}$

To do a multiple integral, add more arguments to the **Integrate** command. This command gives the integral with respect to **y**, then with respect to **x** (note that the first variable named is done last):

```
Integrate[x^2 y^3, x, y]
```

$\frac{x^3 y^4}{12}$

The same order applies to differentiation:

```
D[x^2 y^3, x, y]
```

6 x y²

You can do derivatives involving undefined functions of the variable. For example, this is a basic use of the chain rule:

```
D[u[v[x]], x]
```

u'[v[x]] v'[x]

The notation **v' [x]** means the first derivative of **v** with respect to **x**. Since we haven't defined **v** to be any specific function, its derivative can't be evaluated further.

Here is an example of the product rule with three functions:

```
D[u[x] v[x] w[x], x]
```

```
v[x] w[x] u'[x] + u[x] w[x] v'[x] + u[x] v[x] w'[x]
```

There are other ways of specifying which elements of the expression should be treated as constants and which should be assumed to depend on the variable. See The *Mathematica* Book for more information.

Although it is easy to differentiate any function using only a few simple rules, most integrals are very hard or impossible to do. *Mathematica* has a relatively good integrator (see The *Mathematica* Book for more details about what kinds of functions can and can't be integrated).

Mathematica can integrate rational functions (that is, the quotient of two polynomials):

```
Integrate[x^5 / (x^3 + 3 x^2 + 7 x), x]
```

$$2 x - \frac{3 x^2}{2} + \frac{x^3}{3} - \frac{73 \text{ ArcTan}[\frac{3 + 2 x}{\text{Sqrt}[19]}]}{\text{Sqrt}[19]} +$$
$$\frac{15 \text{ Log}[7 + 3 x + x^2]}{2}$$

It can integrate many other kinds of functions:

```
Integrate[Sin[x]^2, x]
```

$$\frac{x}{2} - \frac{\text{Sin}[2 x]}{4}$$

It recognizes many integrals that can be defined in terms of special functions:

```
Integrate[a b^(-x^2), x]
```

$$\frac{a \text{ Sqrt}[Pi] \text{ Erf}[x \text{ Sqrt}[Log[b]]]}{2 \text{ Sqrt}[Log[b]]}$$

```
Integrate[Sin[x^2]^2, x]
```

$$\frac{2\ x\ -\ \text{Sqrt[Pi]}\ \text{FresnelC}[\frac{2\ x}{\text{Sqrt[Pi]}}]}{4}$$

```
Integrate[Sin[x^2] / x^5, x]
```

$$\frac{-\text{Cos}[x^2]}{4\ x^2}\ -\ \frac{\text{Sin}[x^2]}{4\ x^4}\ -\ \frac{\text{SinIntegral}[x^2]}{4}$$

Note: If you are using a Macintosh, MS Windows, or MS-DOS version of *Mathematica*, doing complex integrals like the ones above may cause *Mathematica* to load a package before the integral is done. This loading is done automatically, and the only thing you will notice is an additional delay the first time an integral of this type is done. Be warned, however, that loading the package can take over one megabyte of memory and may not be possible on smaller computers.

When *Mathematica* can't do an integral, it returns the command unevaluated:

```
Integrate[Cos[Cos[x]], x]
```

```
Integrate[Cos[Cos[x]], x]
```

Mathematica can also do definite integration:

```
Integrate[x^3, {x, 0, 1}]
```

$$\frac{1}{4}$$

It can do improper definite integrals:

```
Integrate[a b^-x^2, {x, 0, Infinity}]
```

$$\frac{a\ \text{Sqrt[Pi]}}{2\ \text{Sqrt[Log[b]]}}$$

As with indefinite integrals, when *Mathematica* can't do a definite integral, it returns the command unevaluated:

```
Integrate[Cos[Cos[x]], {x, 0, 1}]
```
```
Integrate[Cos[Cos[x]], {x, 0, 1}]
```

You can use **N** to compute the integral numerically:

```
N[Integrate[Cos[Cos[x]], {x, 0, 1}]]
```
```
0.659781
```

If you know you want to do the integration numerically, you can use **NIntegrate**. This prevents *Mathematica* from *trying* to do the integration symbolically first:

```
NIntegrate[Cos[Cos[x]], {x, 0, 1}]
```
```
0.659781
```

You might think that indefinite integrals can't be computed numerically, because the answer is a function, not a number. But just as you can have a numerical approximation of a number, in *Mathematica* you can also have a numerical approximation of a function (called an **InterpolatingFunction**).

To compute an indefinite integral numerically, you have to use **NDSolve**, not **Integrate**. The following example computes and then plots the indefinite numerical integral of **Cos[Cos[x]]**, over a range from **-10** to **10**.

```
NDSolve[{y'[x] == Cos[Cos[x]], y[0] == 0}, y[x],
    {x, -10, 10}]
```

```
{{y[x] -> InterpolatingFunction[{-10., 10.}, <>][x]}}
```

```
Plot[y[x] /. %, {x, -10, 10}];
```

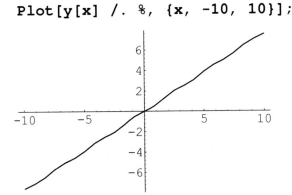

You can use this example as a template. Replace `Cos[Cos[x]]` with your function, and `-10, 10` with the range over which you want the result to be valid. If you want to know more about how `NDSolve` works, see Chapter 21, "How do I solve differential equations?".

■ Worked Example

Jerry: Most calculus textbooks have a section in which they plot a function, then they plot its derivative, then its second derivative, etc. Can we do this?

Theo: The following commands will make such plots. (Plotting is explained in more detail in the plotting chapters in this book, so we won't go into any detail here.) We use the notation `D[f, {x, 2}]`, which means differentiate with respect to **x** twice. (Don't worry about what **Evaluate** means; for now just type it in and use it.)

To make plots of your own favorite function, change the definition in the first line (we're going to look at **x^3**):

```
f = x^3;
Plot[f, {x, -3, 3}];
Plot[Evaluate[D[f, x]], {x, -3, 3}];
Plot[Evaluate[D[f, {x, 2}]], {x, -3, 3}];
```

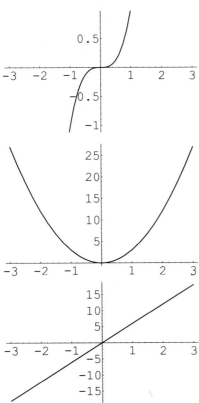

Jerry: What if I want to see all three on the same set of axes?

Theo: Use the following command:

```
f = x^3;
Plot[Evaluate[{f, D[f, x],D[f, {x, 2}]}], {x,-3,3}];
```

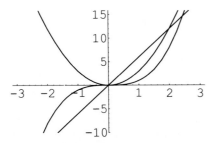

Jerry: How would I make a table of derivatives of a function?

Theo: Here's a nice little command that makes a formatted table of derivatives (again, change the definition of **f** to whatever function you like):

```
f = x^6 + Sin[x];
Do[
   Print[
      n,
      Switch[n,0,"th",1,"st",2,"nd",3,"rd",_,"th"],
      " Derivative = ",
      D[f, {x, n}]
   ],
   {n, 0, 10}
]
```

$$0\text{th Derivative} = x^6 + \operatorname{Sin}[x]$$
$$1\text{st Derivative} = 6 x^5 + \operatorname{Cos}[x]$$
$$2\text{nd Derivative} = 30 x^4 - \operatorname{Sin}[x]$$
$$3\text{rd Derivative} = 120 x^3 - \operatorname{Cos}[x]$$
$$4\text{th Derivative} = 360 x^2 + \operatorname{Sin}[x]$$
$$5\text{th Derivative} = 720 x + \operatorname{Cos}[x]$$
$$6\text{th Derivative} = 720 - \operatorname{Sin}[x]$$
$$7\text{th Derivative} = -\operatorname{Cos}[x]$$
$$8\text{th Derivative} = \operatorname{Sin}[x]$$
$$9\text{th Derivative} = \operatorname{Cos}[x]$$
$$10\text{th Derivative} = -\operatorname{Sin}[x]$$

You can ignore the tricky **Switch** command, it's just to make the output look pretty.

■ Worked Example

Jerry: The product rule is usually seen with two functions:

```
D[u[x] v[x], x]
```

```
v[x] u'[x] + u[x] v'[x]
```

My interest increases if there are three or more functions involved:

```
D[u[x] v[x] w[x], x]
```

```
v[x] w[x] u'[x] + u[x] w[x] v'[x] + u[x] v[x] w'[x]
```

```
D[u[x] v[x] w[x] y[x], x]
```

```
v[x] w[x] y[x] u'[x] + u[x] w[x] y[x] v'[x] +
    u[x] v[x] y[x] w'[x] + u[x] v[x] w[x] y'[x]
```

From this we can see that there is a fairly simple general pattern.

Chapter 20
How do I find limits?

To calculate the limit of a function, use the **Limit** command. For example:

```
Limit[Sin[x] / x, x -> 0]
1
```

• The first argument is the function to take the limit of.
• The second argument specifies the variable to use and the value to approach. The notation **x   -> 0** should be read as "**x** goes to **0**".

In some cases, when you approach a limit from different directions, you get different limiting values. You can specify a direction using the **Direction** option. The following command calculates the limit approaching from the left (that is, traveling towards the right, or in a positive direction):

```
Limit[Tan[x], x -> Pi/2, Direction -> 1]
Infinity
```

The next example approaches from the right. Note that the value you give **Direction** indicates what direction you want to travel in, not where you are coming from. Thus a negative value means traveling in the negative direction, or from the right. Only the sign is important, not the magnitude (the number can be complex, in which case only the phase is important).

```
Limit[Tan[x], x -> Pi/2, Direction -> -1]
-Infinity
```

You can use **Limit** to calculate derivatives, just like they did before television was invented:

```
g[x_] := x^2;
Limit[(g[x + dx] - g[x]) / dx, dx -> 0]
```

```
2 x
```

To try this with your own function, change the definition of **g[x_]** in the command above.

■ Worked Example

Jerry: I've heard from many people who have gotten wrong answers from many different mathematics programs. Although I'm sure these programs will all be perfect in their next versions, can we trust them now?

Theo: You should never *really* trust the result of any single calculation, whether done by a computer program or by a human. If you're going to build a bridge, check your work at least twice before you let the mayor cut the ribbon, or you may end up the laughing stock of future bridge-building classes.

Jerry: For example, if we have any doubts about a symbolic limit, it's always a good idea to try making some plots and calculating a few numerical values around the limit. That way we can see if the claimed limit makes any sense. Let's try an example:

```
Limit[(1 - Cos[x^2]) / x^4, x -> 0]
```

$$\frac{1}{2}$$

Does this make sense? Let's make a plot:

```
Plot[(1 - Cos[x^2]) / x^4, {x, -5, 5}];
```

From the plot it's certainly reasonable to think that the limit might be 1/2. Let's try substituting a few values near zero:

```
(1 - Cos[x^2]) / x^4 /. x->0.1
0.499996

(1 - Cos[x^2]) / x^4 /. x->0.01
0.5

(1 - Cos[x^2]) / x^4 /. x->0.0001
0.499817

(1 - Cos[x^2]) / x^4 /. x->0.000001
0.
```

This looks looks strange. It seems to be close to 1/2, but then it suddenly becomes zero.

Theo: This is probably caused by numerical round off. Let's try the same expression but with more decimal places. (*Mathematica* notices how many decimal places you start with and preserves accuracy in the course of the calculation.)

```
(1 - Cos[x^2]) / x^4 /.
     x -> 0.000001000000000000000000000000000000000000
0.499999999999999999999999958333333
```

Jerry: So, it looks as if in this case *Mathematica* most likely did get the correct exact answer, since the numerical values do seem to approach 1/2.

Theo: Naturally this is not a proof of anything, but this sort of sanity check is a good idea if the result really matters.

Chapter 21
How do I solve differential equations?

The function **DSolve** solves symbolic differential equations in much the same way that **Solve** solves algebraic equations. The function **NDSolve**, described later in this chapter, solves differential equations numerically.

Here is an example of **DSolve**:

```
DSolve[y'[x] == x^2, y[x], x]
```

$$\{\{y[x] \; -> \; \frac{x^3}{3} \; + \; C[1]\}\}$$

- The first argument is the equation to be solved, written in terms of a function (**y[x]**) and its derivatives (**y'[x]**, **y''[x]**, etc.).
- The second argument is the function to be solved for.
- The third argument is the independent variable.

The result is given as a list of replacement rules. See Chapter 18, "How do I solve equations?", for more information about how to read and use results in this form (**C[1]** represents an arbitrary constant of integration).

You can give **DSolve** a list of equations as its first argument and it will solve them simultaneously. This is useful for specifying initial conditions and/or boundary conditions:

```
DSolve[{y'[x] == x^2, y[0] == 1}, y[x], x]
```

$$\{\{y[x] \; -> \; 1 \; + \; \frac{x^3}{3}\}\}$$

DSolve can solve a wide variety of differential equations; here are a few examples:

```
DSolve[y''[x] + y[x] == 0, y[x], x]
```
```
{{y[x] -> C[2] Cos[x] - C[1] Sin[x]}}
```
```
DSolve[{y''[x] + y[x] == 0, y''[0] == 0}, y[x], x]
```
```
{{y[x] -> -(C[1] Sin[x])}}
```
```
DSolve[{y''[x] + y[x]==0, y''[0]==0, y[Pi/2]==1},
    y[x], x]
```
```
{{y[x] -> Sin[x]}}
```
```
DSolve[{x y'[x] == 3 y[x] + x^4 Cos[x], y[2Pi] == 0},
    y[x], x]
```
$$\{\{y[x] \rightarrow x^3\ Sin[x]\}\}$$
```
DSolve[{y'[x] + y[x] == E^x, y[0] == 1}, y[x], x]
```
$$\{\{y[x] \rightarrow \frac{1}{2\ E^x} + \frac{E^x}{2}\}\}$$

DSolve can also solve systems of equations involving more than one function. In such cases you give **DSolve** a list of functions as its second argument instead of a single function:

```
DSolve[{u'[x]==v[x], v'[x]==u[x]}, {u[x], v[x]}, x]
```
$$\{\{u[x] \rightarrow \frac{C[1] + E^{2\ x}\ C[1] - C[2] + E^{2\ x}\ C[2]}{2\ E^x},$$
$$v[x] \rightarrow \frac{-C[1] + E^{2\ x}\ C[1] + C[2] + E^{2\ x}\ C[2]}{2\ E^x}\}\}$$

There are a number of additional features and capabilities of **DSolve**; anyone using it extensively should read about them in The *Mathematica* Book.

NDSolve allows you to solve differential equations numerically. This function takes the same arguments as **DSolve**, with a few extra restrictions. You must specify enough initial conditions to give completely determined solutions, and all the conditions must be specified at the same value of the independent variable. You must also specify a numerical range for the independent variable (this is the range over which the solution will be valid). Here is an example:

```
NDSolve[{y'[x] == x^2, y[0] == 1}, y[x], {x, -1, 1}]
    {{y[x] -> InterpolatingFunction[{-1., 1.}, <>][x]}}
```

- The first argument is the system of equations to be solved.
- The second argument is the function to solve for.
- The third argument is a standard range specification list, indicating that the independent variable, **x**, should run from **-1** to **1**.

The result is given in the same format as for **Solve** or **DSolve**, except that the solution is an **InterpolatingFunction** object. An **Interpolating-Function** is like a black box; given an input value it produces an output, but you can't see anything of its internal structure. Usually the best thing to do with an **InterpolatingFunction** is to plot it.

The first step in plotting the solution is to extract the **Interpolating-Functions** from the result of the **NDSolve** command. This is done in much the same way as one extracts results from a **Solve** command (see Chapter 18, "How do I solve equations?", for more information):

```
solutions = y[x] /.
    NDSolve[{y'[x]==x^2, y[0]==1}, y[x], {x, -1, 1}]
    {InterpolatingFunction[{-1., 1.}, <>][x]}
```

Now we can plot the solution (but only over the range that was originally specified for the solution):

Plot[solutions, {x, -1, 1}];

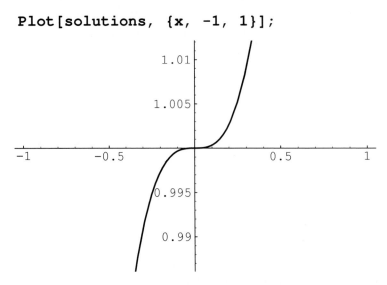

In this case we could have solved the equation symbolically using **DSolve**, but there are many differential equations that can be solved only numerically. As with **DSolve**, there are many more features and capabilities of **NDSolve**. The interested reader should consult The *Mathematica* Book.

Chapter 22
How do I plot a function in two dimensions?

There are many plotting commands in *Mathematica*, but to plot functions in two dimensions you need only **Plot**:

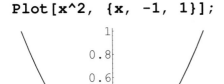

```
Plot[x^2, {x, -1, 1}];
```

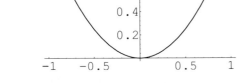

- The first argument is the expression to be plotted.
- The second argument tells *Mathematica* to use the variable **x** and let it run from **-1** to **1**.

Mathematica chooses the vertical axis range automatically, and it chooses enough sample points to make the curve smooth. All these parameters can be adjusted using options (see The *Mathematica* Book for information).

If you plot a function with extreme values, such as the trig function
Tan[x], *Mathematica* tries to pick a reasonable vertical range:

    Plot[Tan[x], {x, -2, 2}];

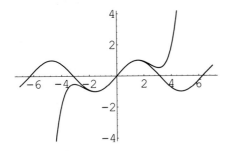

You can plot two or more functions on the same set of axes by using a list
as the first argument to the **Plot** command:

    Plot[{Sin[x], x - x^3/6 + x^5/120}, {x, -7, 7}];

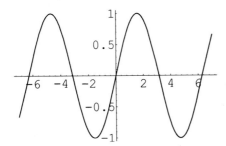

You can change the color and/or dashing pattern of the curve using the
PlotStyle option. The following curve will be blue on a color computer:

    Plot[Sin[x], {x, -7, 7}, PlotStyle -> Hue[2/3]];

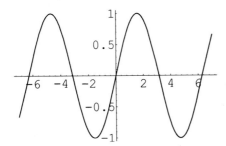

See Figure 3 on the back cover for a color version.

The following curve has a regular dashing pattern. Its dashes and spaces are equal in length to 0.05 times the width of the plot:

```
Plot[Sin[x], {x,-7,7}, PlotStyle->Dashing[{0.05}]];
```

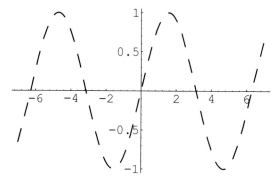

If you have more than one curve on the same axes, you can distinguish them using color and/or dashing pattern. In the following example the first element of the **PlotStyle** list applies to the first expression in the **Plot** command, etc.:

```
Plot[{Sin[x], x - x^3/6 + x^5/120}, {x, -7, 7},
     PlotStyle -> {Hue[2/3], Hue[1/3]}];
```

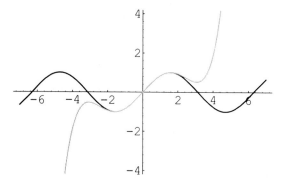

See Figure 6 on the back cover for a color version.

You can label the plot using the **PlotLabel** option:

```
Plot[Sin[x], {x, 0, 2Pi},
   PlotLabel -> "The Sine Function"];
```

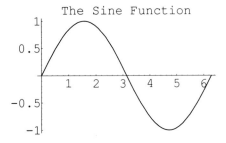

You can label the axes using the **AxesLabel** option:

```
Plot[Sin[x], {x, 0, 2Pi},
   AxesLabel -> {"x", "Sin[x]"}];
```

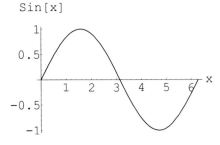

You can put a frame around the whole plot:

```
Plot[Sin[x], {x, 0, 2Pi},
   Frame -> True];
```

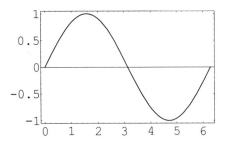

You can superimpose grid lines (by default, blue):

```
Plot[Sin[x], {x, 0, 2Pi},
   Frame -> True,
   GridLines -> Automatic];
```

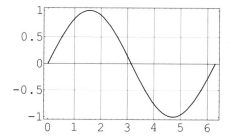

You can change the fonts used in the plot. Fonts are specified as a list: The first element is the font name, and the second element is the point size. In the next example we specify a font to use for all text in the plot:

```
Plot[Sin[x], {x, 0, 2Pi},
   DefaultFont -> {"Helvetica", 18}];
```

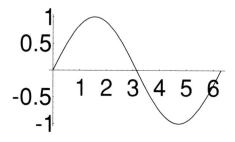

The naming of fonts is a very delicate issue. *Mathematica* uses PostScript to generate all its graphics, so fonts must be named in the PostScript way. This is not always the same way fonts are named in other programs on your computer. For example to get an *Italic Times* font, you need to use "Times-Italic", but to get an *Italic Helvetica* you have to use "Helvetica-Oblique". In general it is impossible to predict how any given font will handle style variations: You have to look it up in an Adobe font catalog.

To change the font of an individual text element (label, tick mark, etc.), use the **FontForm** command. **FontForm** takes two arguments: First the text or expression to be displayed, and second a font specification.

```
Plot[Sin[x], {x, 0, 2Pi}, PlotLabel -> FontForm[
        "The Sine Function",
        {"Times-BoldItalic", 18}]];
```

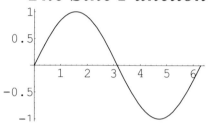

Of course, these options can be combined in the same plot. (Some options don't go well together. For example, **AxesLabel** is not useful combined with **Frame->True**, because there are no axes when there is a frame. Use **FrameLabel** instead.)

```
Plot[Sin[x], {x, 0, 2Pi}, PlotStyle->Thickness[0.01],
    Frame -> True, GridLines -> Automatic,
    PlotLabel -> FontForm["The Sine Function",
        {"ZapfChancery-MediumItalic", 24}],
    FrameLabel->{FontForm["x",{"Palatino-Italic",18}],
        FontForm["Sin[x]",{"Palatino-Italic", 18}]},
    DefaultFont -> {"Helvetica-Oblique", 14}];
```

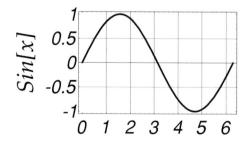

Mathematica normally displays all plots with an aspect ratio (ratio of height/width) of about 1/1.6 (one over the Golden Ratio). Sometimes you may want to override this, which you can do using the **AspectRatio** option. For example, the following plot looks crowded:

Plot[Sin[x], {x, 0, 40Pi}];

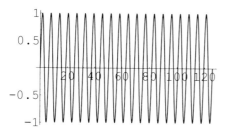

It would look better displayed in a wide, short area (that is, with a smaller aspect ratio):

Plot[Sin[x], {x, 0, 40Pi}, AspectRatio -> 0.2];

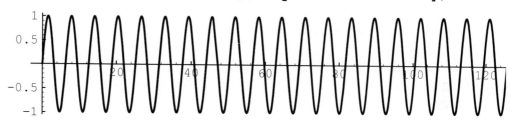

In the following example, the physical slope of the line is different from what we might expect from the equation:

Plot[2 x, {x, 0, 5}];

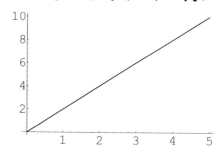

This is because the default aspect ratio gives us scales that are different in the horizontal and vertical directions. The setting **AspectRatio -> Automatic** tells *Mathematica* to use the same scale in both directions:

>   Plot[2 x, {x, 0, 5}, AspectRatio -> Automatic];

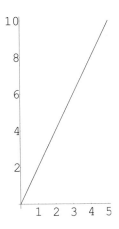

■ Worked Example

Jerry: Many graphing programs have a Zoom feature that allows you to magnify a plot around some chosen point. How do we do this in *Mathematica*?

Theo: By changing the numbers in the **Plot** command. Start with this plot:

>   Plot[{Sin[x], Cos[x]}, {x, 0, 2Pi}];

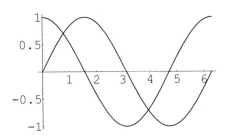

You might like to look closely at the point where the lines cross, so you change the **x** range:

Plot[{Sin[x], Cos[x]}, {x, 0.7, 0.9}];

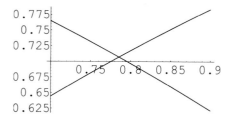

Jerry: How did you choose those two values, **0.7** and **0.9**?

Theo: I used the coordinate display feature in the Notebook front end. To use this feature, click on a graph. A bounding box will appear around the graph. Hold down the Command key (Macintosh or NeXT) or the Alt key (DOS) and move the mouse over the graph. You will see the coordinates of where you are pointing displayed at the bottom of the window.

Jerry: That's nice. I suppose you could use the same feature to see where the curves cross.

I like using the option **AspectRatio -> Automatic** because circles look like circles, not ovals. The slopes of straight lines also look correct. Why isn't this option set by default?

Theo: Try plotting **8 x**. *Most* plots are likely to be much too tall or much too wide with an automatic aspect ratio.

Chapter 23
How do I plot a parametric equation in two dimensions?

The **ParametricPlot** command is much like the **Plot** command:

```
ParametricPlot[{t^2, t}, {t, -2, 2}];
```

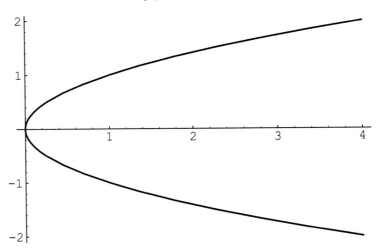

- The first argument is a list of two functions that specify the x and y coordinates as a function of the single parameter, **t**. Here x is **t^2** and y is **t**.
- The second argument specifies the range of the parameter, here **t** goes from **-2** to **2**.

If you want to plot more than one parametric equation on the same set of axes, you can give **ParametricPlot** a list of two lists of functions. For example:

ParametricPlot[{{t^3, t^2}, {t^2, t^3}}, {t, -2, 2}];

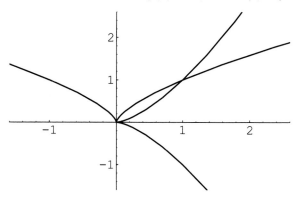

Most of the options that can be used with **Plot** (explained in Chapter 22, "How do I plot a function in two dimensions?") can also be used with **ParametricPlot**. For example, the option **AspectRatio -> Automatic** can be used to force the horizontal and vertical directions to be scaled uniformly:

ParametricPlot[{{t^3, t^2}, {t^2, t^3}}, {t, -2, 2}, AspectRatio -> Automatic];

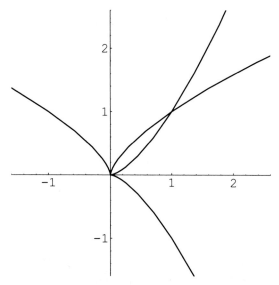

The option **PlotStyle** can be used, for example, to draw one of the curves dashed:

```
ParametricPlot[{{t^3, t^2}, {t^2, t^3}}, {t, -2, 2},
    AspectRatio -> Automatic,
    PlotStyle -> {{}, Dashing[{0.02}]}];
```

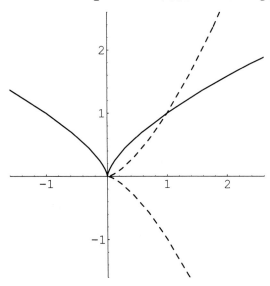

Many people use parametric plots when they want to plot nonfunctions (like the first example in this chapter, which is not a function because a vertical line at any positive value of *x* will intersect two branches). An alternative approach is to use implicit plot, described in Chapter 25, "How do I plot implicitly defined functions?".

See The *Mathematica* Book or Chapter 22, "How do I plot a function in two dimensions?", for more information about plotting options.

Chapter 24
How do I plot in polar coordinates?

To make a polar plot, you first need to execute the following command:

```
Needs["Graphics`Graphics`"];
```

(Note that the two single quotes used here are "back quotes" usually found on the same key with ~. They are *not* the single quotes found on the double-quote key.)

The command loads in the standard package `Graphics.m`, which is included in all copies of *Mathematica* Version 2. The package contains definitions for a variety of useful graphics functions, including **PolarPlot**.

PolarPlot is similar to **Plot**:

```
PolarPlot[t, {t, 0, 2Pi}];
```

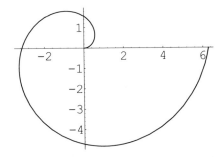

- The first argument is the radial function.
- The second argument specifies the range of the angular variable **t**, in this case from **0** to **2Pi**.

If you want to plot more than one function on the same set of axes, you can
give **PolarPlot** a list of functions as its first argument:

PolarPlot[{t, t^1.1, t^1.2}, {t, 0, 2Pi}];

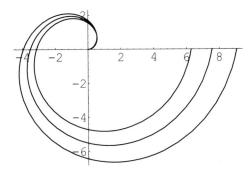

PolarPlot automatically makes the horizontal and vertical scales equal.
This is so that a circle like the following one looks like a circle, not an oval:

PolarPlot[1, {t, 0, 2Pi}];

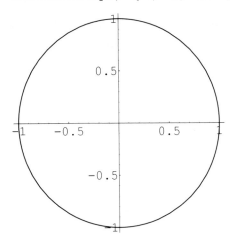

PolarPlot can take most of the same options as **Plot**. See The *Mathematica* Book or Chapter 22, "How do I plot a function in two dimensions?", for
more information about plotting options.

The coordinate display feature described in Chapter 22 also works for
plots generated by **PolarPlot**, but the points will be displayed in
Cartesian coordinates, not polar ones.

Chapter 25
How do I plot implicitly defined functions?

To make plots of implicitly defined functions, you first need to execute the following command:

```
Needs["Graphics`ImplicitPlot`"];
```

(Note that the two single quotes used here are "back quotes" usually found on the same key with ~. They are *not* the single quotes found on the double-quote key.)

The command loads in the standard package ImplicitPlot.m, which is included in all copies of *Mathematica* Version 2. This package defines the function **ImplicitPlot** (written by Jerry Keiper and based on an idea by Dan Grayson).

ImplicitPlot is similar to **Plot**, except that instead of an expression involving only one variable, you give it an equation involving two variables (conventionally **x** and **y**). Here is an example:

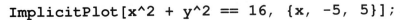

```
ImplicitPlot[x^2 + y^2 == 16, {x, -5, 5}];
```

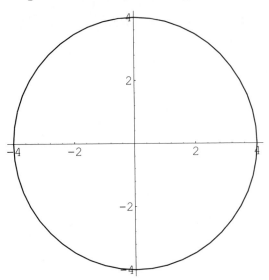

• The first argument is the equation to be plotted. Note that in *Mathematica* equality is denoted by a double-equal symbol (**==**).

• The second argument gives the range of the horizontal variable. *Mathematica* automatically chooses a suitable range for the other variable.

Here are a few more examples that can be made with this command.

The ellipse:

```
ImplicitPlot[x^2 + 2 y^2 == 3, {x, -2, 2}];
```

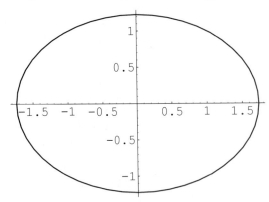

The lemniscate:

```
ImplicitPlot[(x^2 + y^2)^2==(x^2 - y^2), {x,-2,2}];
```

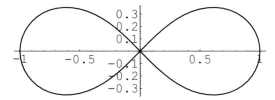

The folium of Descartes:

```
ImplicitPlot[x^3 + y^3 == 3 x y, {x, -3, 3}];
```

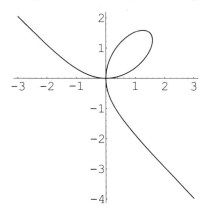

You can plot two equations on the same set of axes by giving **Implicit-Plot** a list of two equations as its first argument:

```
ImplicitPlot[{
    (x^2 + y^2)^2 == (x^2 - y^2),
    (x^2 + y^2)^2 == 2 x y},
    {x, -2, 2}];
```

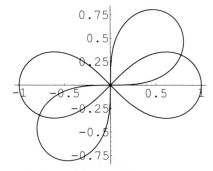

The **PlotStyle** option can be used to distinguish the curves from each other. **PlotStyle** is explained in Chapter 22, "How do I plot a function in two dimensions?".

```
ImplicitPlot[{
    (x^2 + y^2)^2 == (x^2 - y^2),
    (x^2 + y^2)^2 == 2 x y},
   {x, -2, 2},
   PlotStyle -> {Dashing[{}], Dashing[{.01}]}];
```

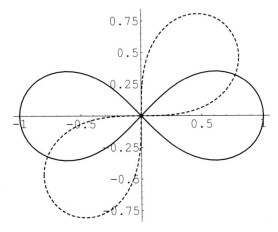

When used in the form described so far, **ImplicitPlot** must be able to solve the equations for one or the other variable. In certain cases this is not possible, for example:

```
ImplicitPlot[x^y == y^x, {x, 0, 5}]
```

Solve::dinv:

The expression x^y involves unknowns in more than one argument, so inverse functions can't be used.

ImplicitPlot::epfail:

Equation $x^y == y^x$ could not be solved for points to plot.

ImplicitPlot[x^y == y^x, {x, 0, 5}]

In cases such as this, you can make **ImplicitPlot** use a completely different technique by giving it a third argument that specifies the range for the second variable. For example:

ImplicitPlot[x^y == y^x, {x, 0, 5}, {y, 0, 5}];

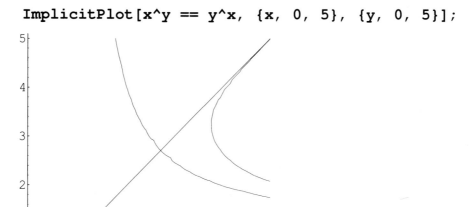

When used in this form, **ImplicitPlot** does not try to solve the equations. Instead it evaluates both sides on a regular grid across the *x-y* plane, and draws lines along where the difference between the two sides changed sign. (It uses the built-in function **ContourPlot** to do this. The interested reader should consult The *Mathematica* Book for more information about **ContourPlot**. Options added to **ImplicitPlot** will be passed on to **ContourPlot**.)

Generally, the three-argument form of **ImplicitPlot** is quite slow and produces plots with nonsmooth curves. On the other hand, the three-argument form is able to plot just about any equation, including many that the two-argument form can't. So it is often sensible to try the two-argument form first, and if that doesn't work, switch to the three-argument form.

Chapter 26
How do I show the area between curves?

To show the area between two curves (or the area between one curve and the x-axis), you first need to execute the following command:

Needs["Graphics`FilledPlot`"];

(Note that the two single quotes used here are "back quotes" usually found on the same key with ~. They are *not* the single quotes found on the double-quote key.)

The command loads in the standard package `FilledPlot.m`, which is included in all copies of *Mathematica* Version 2. The package defines **FilledPlot** (written by John M. Novak).

FilledPlot is similar to **Plot**. The following command plots the area between **x^2** and the *x* axis:

FilledPlot[x^2, {x, -2, 2}];

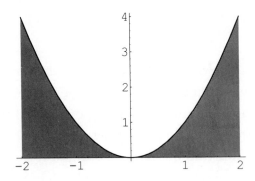

- The first argument is the expression to be plotted.
- The second argument tells *Mathematica* to use the variable **x** and let it run from **-2** to **2**.

If we give **FilledPlot** a list of two elements as its first argument, the resulting plot shows the area between these two curves.

FilledPlot[{x, x^2}, {x, -1, 2}];

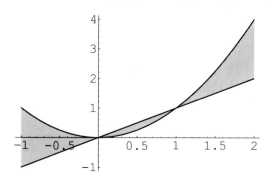

Note that both positive and negative areas are shown.

Here are some more examples:

FilledPlot[{Abs[x], Sin[x]}, {x, -2, 2}];

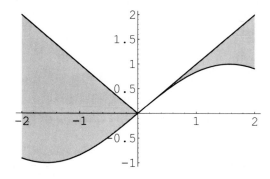

```
FilledPlot[{(x^2-4)/(x-2), Sin[x]},   {x, -5, 2}];
```

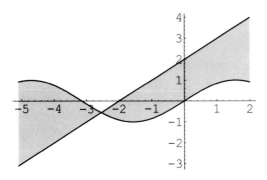

You can give **FilledPlot** a list of more than two functions, and the areas between successive functions will be colored automatically.

```
FilledPlot[{x, x^2, x^3, x^4}, {x, -1, 2}];
```

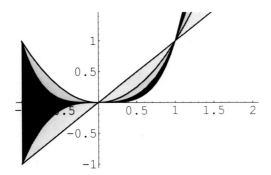

FilledPlot can take most of the same options that **Plot** can: See Chapter 22, "How do I plot a function in two dimensions?", or The *Mathematica* Book for more information. **FilledPlot** also has several options unique to it: See the standard package documentation that comes with each copy of *Mathematica* Version 2 for more information.

Chapter 27
How do I plot a function in three dimensions?

Plotting in three dimensions is one of the great pleasures of *Mathematica*.
The only command you need to know in order to plot functions of two
variables in three dimensions is **Plot3D**:

```
Plot3D[x^3 + y^3, {x, -2, 2}, {y, -3, 3}];
```

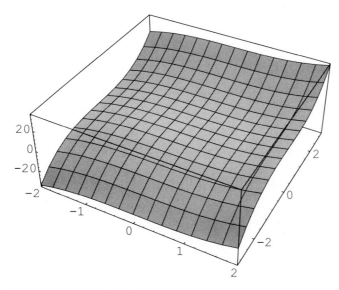

See Figure 5 on the back cover for a color version.

- The first argument is the expression to be plotted.
- The second argument says use **x** as one variable, going from **-2** to **2**.
- The third argument says use **y** as the other variable, going from **-3** to **3**.

By default the function is plotted on a 15 by 15 grid, and each patch is colored according to a simple reflected-light model (more details in the "Coloring" section later in this chapter).

Mathematica puts 3D plots in a box. The orientation of this box is determined by the viewpoint from which it is being observed. With the default viewpoint, the orientation has the following features:

• The x scale is roughly horizontal in the front left, with x values increasing to the right.
• The y scale runs roughly front to back on the right, with y values increasing to the back.
• The z scale runs vertically on the left, with *z values increasing upward*.

This means that the x-y plane in the plot is seen about the same way it is if you lay a piece of x-y graph paper on a table in front of you, with the y axis increasing away from you and the x axis increasing to the right. (Some programs that make 3D plots choose a default viewpoint such that the x axis increases from the back to the front left, and the y axis increases from the back to the front right.) With *Mathematica*'s default viewpoint, it is easy to go from a 2D plot to a 3D plot to see how they relate to each other.

All the features described above can be changed using options for the **Plot3D** command. A few of these options are described below; the rest are described in The *Mathematica* Book.

■ Number of plot points

Here is an example of a plot that does not come out very well with the default settings:

```
Plot3D[Sin[x Sin[x y]], {x, 0, 4}, {y, 0, 3}];
```

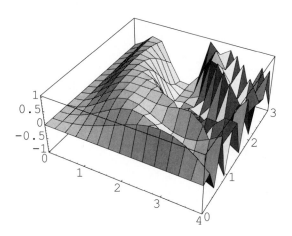

The left side is reasonable, but it's hard to tell what's happening on the right side. We can use the **PlotPoints** option to help resolve the shape:

```
Plot3D[Sin[x Sin[x y]], {x, 0, 4}, {y, 0, 3},
    PlotPoints -> 50];
```

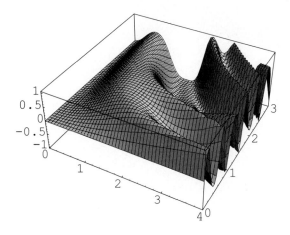

See Figure 4 on the back cover for a color version.

The grid has been increased from the default 15 by 15 to 50 by 50.

At this point we should warn you that making 3D plots with a large number of plot points can require a *very* large amount of memory! Try making a variety of different 3D plots to learn how large a plot you can make with your particular computer. Try a simple plot first, and increase the plot points until things stop working well.

■ Viewpoint

The following plot is a little hard to decipher (**Zeta** means the Riemann Zeta function):

```
Plot3D[Abs[Zeta[y + x I]],
    {x, 1, 60}, {y, -1, 1},
    PlotPoints -> 40];
```

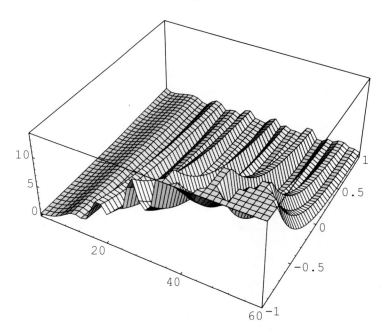

Changing to a different viewpoint helps us to see it better:

```
Plot3D[Abs[Zeta[y + x I]],
    {x, 1, 60}, {y, -1, 1},
    PlotPoints -> 40,
    ViewPoint->{2.005, 2.664, 0.580}];
```

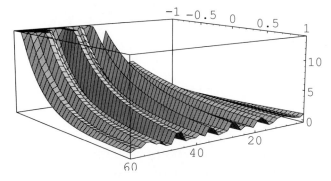

Although you can type in a **ViewPoint** option manually, if you have a Notebook front end you can use the automatic 3D viewpoint selector. The 3D ViewPoint Selector command in the Prepare Input submenu of the Action menu brings up a panel that lets you choose a viewpoint by moving a cube with the mouse. Here is what the panel looks like on a NeXT computer:

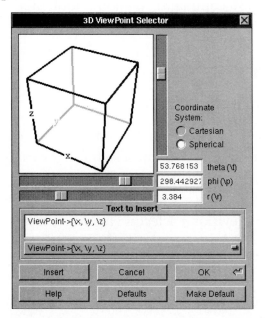

It looks similar on other types of computers.

To use this panel, first type out your **Plot3D** command. For example:

```
Plot3D[x^2 - y^2, {x, -5, 5}, {y, -5, 5}];
```

Add a comma just before the closing square bracket:

```
Plot3D[x^2 - y^2, {x, -5, 5}, {y, -5, 5},];
```

To make the command more readable, you can type a return character, too:

```
Plot3D[x^2 - y^2, {x, -5, 5}, {y, -5, 5},
];
```

Leave the text insertion point (flashing vertical bar) where it is, just before the square bracket, and then open the 3D viewpoint selector (either with the menu, or by using its command-key equivalent, Command-Shift-V).

Click on the cube and hold down the mouse button while moving the mouse around. The cube will rotate in response to your movements. Once you have gotten to a good viewpoint, release the mouse button. Then click the Insert button (NeXT) or the Paste button (Macintosh and MS Windows). The dialog box will be hidden, and an appropriate **ViewPoint** option will be inserted into your **Plot3D** command. It should look like this (with different numbers, depending on the viewpoint you selected):

```
Plot3D[x^2 - y^2, {x, -5, 5}, {y, -5, 5},
ViewPoint->{1.300, -2.400, 2.000}];
```

Now you can evaluate this expression in the normal way.

Note that these instructions assume you are using an unmodified copy of *Mathematica*. It is possible to modify the 3D viewpoint selector in a variety of ways to adapt it to specialized uses (see your user's manual for more information). If you don't get something that looks like the command above, clicking the Defaults button in the 3D viewpoint selector should restore things to normal.

■ Coloring

By default, *Mathematica* colors plots according to a simple lighting model. There are, also by default, three colored lights (red, green, and blue) at three locations. The color of each patch on the surface is determined by the light it reflects to the viewer from each light source. This means that the color depends mainly on the orientation of the patch relative to the lights.

This lighting model sometimes results in poorly colored plots. For example, the first plot in this chapter has a very uniform color across the whole surface (visible in this black-and-white book as a uniform shade of gray). If we add the option **Lighting -> False** to the **Plot3D** command, *Mathematica* will color the plot with shades of gray increasing in brightness as the z value increases:

```
Plot3D[x^3 + y^3, {x, -2, 2}, {y, -3, 3},
     Lighting -> False];
```

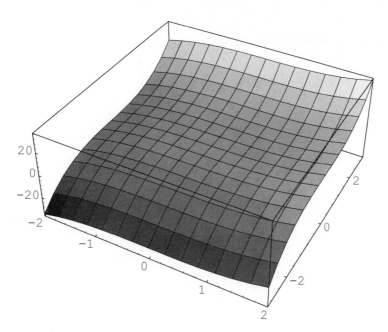

We can also specify the coloring manually for each point on the surface. If the first argument to the **Plot3D** command is a list of two elements, then the first element will be taken as the *z*-value, and the second element will be taken as a color specification. There are many different ways of specifying colors, including **GrayLevel**, **RGBColor**, and **Hue**; they are explained in detail in The *Mathematica* Book. It can be tricky to get a good-looking manual color specification. Here is one:

```
Plot3D[{x^3 + y^3, Hue[(x^3 + y^3)/30]},
    {x, -2, 2}, {y, -3, 3}];
```

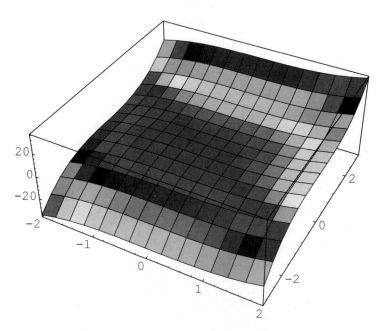

See Figure 1 on the back cover for a color version.

Chapter 28
How do I plot a parametric equation in three dimensions?

There are two forms of **ParametricPlot3D**. Which form to use depends on whether you want space curves or surfaces. To make a space curve, use the following form:

```
ParametricPlot3D[{t, t^3, t^2}, {t, -1, 1}];
```

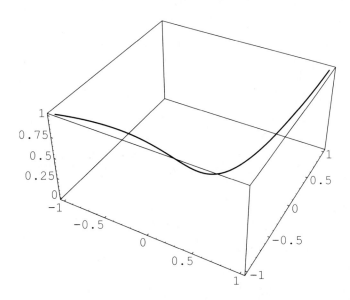

• The first argument is a list of three functions that specify the x, y, and z coordinates as a function of the single parameter, **t**. In this case x is **t**, y is **t^3**, and z is **t^2**.

• The second argument specifies the range of the parameter. In this case **t** goes from **-1** to **1**.

To make a surface, add a second parameter specification:

```
ParametricPlot3D[{u v, u, v},
              {u, -1, 1}, {v, -1, 1}];
```

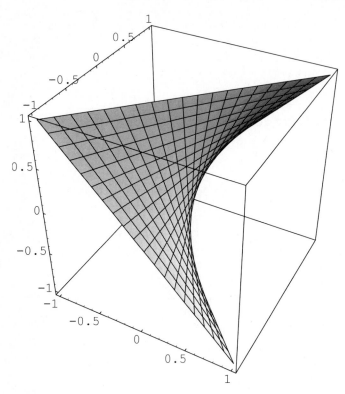

• The first argument is a list of three functions that specify the x, y, and z coordinates as a function of the two parameters, **u** and **v**.
• The second argument specifies the range of the first parameter.
• The third argument specifies the range of the second parameter.

If you want to plot more than one parametric equation on the same set of axes, you can give **ParametricPlot3D** a list of two lists of functions. For example:

```
ParametricPlot3D[{{t, t^3, t^2}, {t^2, t, t^3}},
    {t, -1, 1}];
```

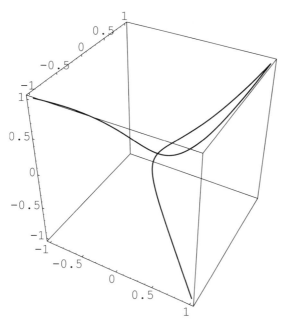

```
ParametricPlot3D[{{u, -v^2, v}, {u, v, u^2 v^2}},
    {u, -1, 1}, {v, -1, 1}];
```

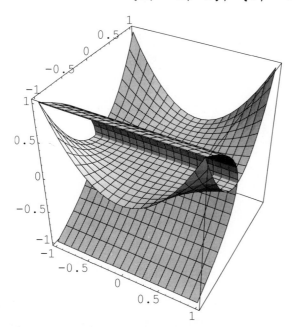

Most of the options that can be used with **Plot3D** (which are explained in Chapter 27, "How do I plot a function in three dimensions?") can also be used with **ParametricPlot3D**. For example, the following options can be used to remove the bounding box and axes:

```
ParametricPlot3D[{{t, t^3, t^2}, {t^2, t, t^3}},
        {t, -1, 1},
        Boxed -> False, Axes -> None];
```

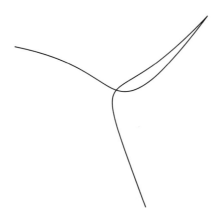

```
ParametricPlot3D[{{u, -v^2, v}, {u, v, u^2 v^2}},
        {u, -1, 1}, {v, -1, 1},
        Boxed -> False, Axes -> None];
```

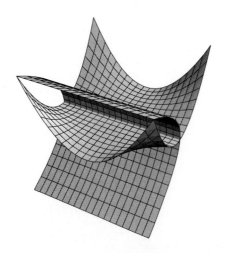

It is OK to have surfaces that intersect themselves. For example:

```
ParametricPlot3D[{v Cos[u], -v Sin[u], u v / 5},
        {u, -3Pi, 3Pi}, {v, -3Pi, 3Pi},
        Boxed -> False, Axes -> None,
        PlotPoints -> {60, 30}];
```

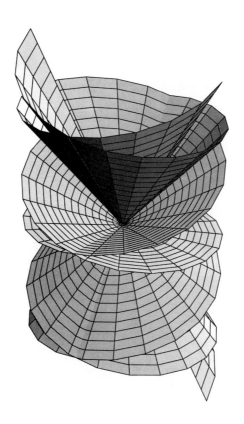

Surfaces that intersect themselves often can take a very long time to render.

Chapter 29
How do I plot in cylindrical and spherical coordinates?

To make a cylindrical or spherical coordinate plot, you first need to execute the following command:

```
Needs["Graphics`ParametricPlot3D`"];
```

(Note that the two single quotes used here are "back quotes" usually found on the same key with ~. They are *not* the single quotes found on the double-quote key.)

This command loads in the standard package `ParametricPlot3D.m`, which is included in all copies of *Mathematica* Version 2. The package contains definitions for a variety of useful graphics functions, including **CylindricalPlot3D** and **SphericalPlot3D**.

CylindricalPlot3D is similar to **Plot3D**:

```
CylindricalPlot3D[r^2 Sin[2 t]/2,
              {r, 0, 1}, {t, 0, 2Pi}];
```

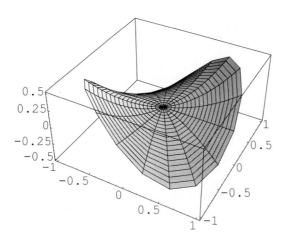

- The first argument gives *z* as a function of radius and angle from *x* axis.
- The second argument gives the radius parameter **r**, going from **0** to **1**.
- The third argument gives the angle parameter **t**, going from **0** to **2Pi**.

You can change the ranges to plot only part of the surface:

```
CylindricalPlot3D[r^2 Sin[2 t]/2,
              {r, .5, 1}, {t, 0, 3Pi/2}];
```

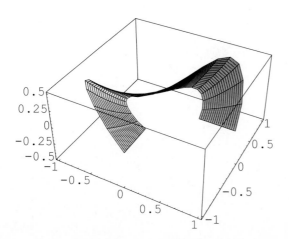

SphericalPlot3D is also similar to **Plot3D**:

```
SphericalPlot3D[2 + Sin[3 t] Sin[3 p],
        {t, 0, Pi}, {p, 0, 2Pi}];
```

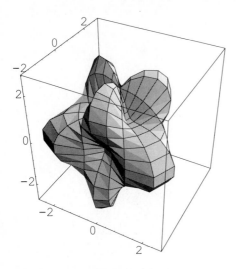

• The first argument gives the radius as a function of theta (**t**) and phi (**p**).

• The second argument gives the range for **t**, the angle from the z axis.

• The third argument gives the range for **p**, the angle from the x axis in the x-y plane.

You can specify only a portion of the full surface:

```
SphericalPlot3D[2 + Sin[3 t] Sin[3 p],
        {t, Pi/2, Pi}, {p, 0, 3Pi/2}];
```

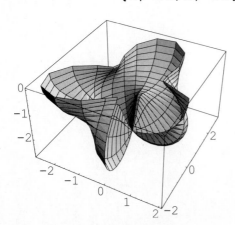

Both **SphericalPlot3D** and **CylindricalPlot3D** can take most of the same options as **Plot3D**, described in Chapter 27, "How do I plot a function in three dimensions?". For example, you can change the number of grid points using the **PlotPoints** option:

```
SphericalPlot3D[2 + Sin[3 t] Sin[3 p],
        {t, 0, Pi}, {p, 0, 2Pi},
        PlotPoints -> {40, 60}];
```

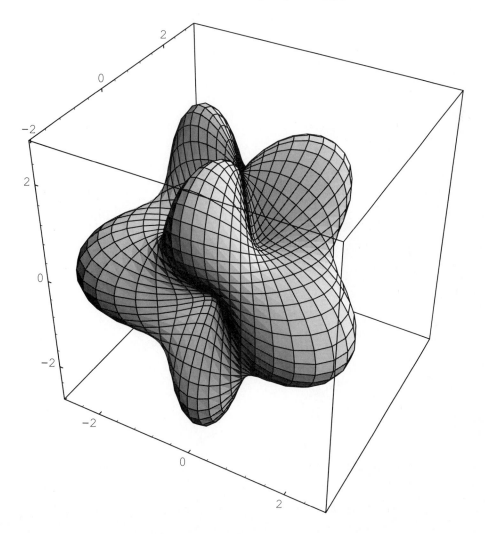

See Figure 2 on the back cover for a color version.

Chapter 30
How do I make contour and density plots?

The functions **Plot3D**, **ContourPlot**, and **DensityPlot** can be used almost interchangeably. Here is the same function plotted with each of these three functions:

```
Plot3D[Sin[x y], {x, 0, 3}, {y, 0, 3}];
```

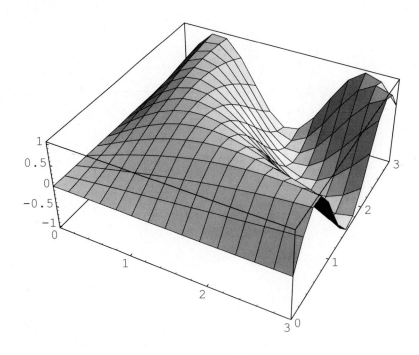

`ContourPlot[Sin[x y], {x, 0, 3}, {y, 0, 3}];`

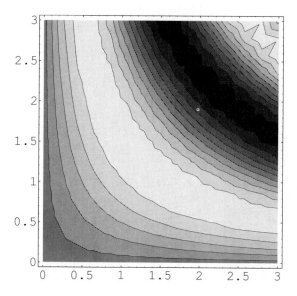

`DensityPlot[Sin[x y], {x, 0, 3}, {y, 0, 3}];`

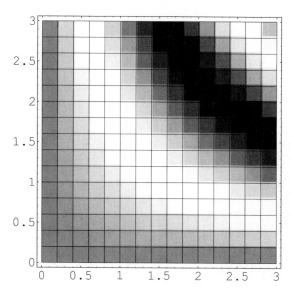

In each case:

- The first argument gives *z* as a function of *x* and *y*.
- The second argument gives the *x* range; in this case from 0 to 3.
- The third argument gives the *y* range; in this case from 0 to 3.

ContourPlot and **DensityPlot** can take most of the same options as **Plot3D**, which are described in Chapter 27, "How do I plot a function in three dimensions?". For example, the **PlotPoints** option can be used to increase the resolution of the plots:

```
ContourPlot[Sin[x y], {x, 0, 3}, {y, 0, 3},
    PlotPoints -> 30];
```

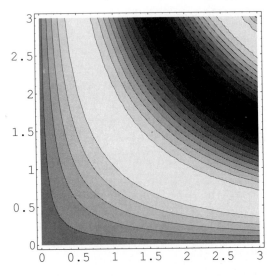

```
DensityPlot[Sin[x y], {x, 0, 3}, {y, 0, 3},
    PlotPoints -> 30];
```

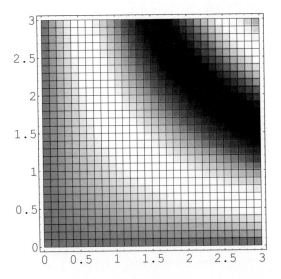

Particularly in the case of **ContourPlot** it is often necessary to adjust several options to get a good-looking plot. See The *Mathematica* Book for more information.

One of the most useful options to use with **DensityPlot** is **Mesh -> False**. This allows us to make much higher resolution plots. Consider this example:

```
DensityPlot[Sin[x/y], {x, -10, 10}, {y, -5, 5},
    PlotPoints -> 500];
```

The mesh lines make this plot almost solid black.

Adding **Mesh -> False** allows us to see the plot:

```
DensityPlot[Sin[x/y], {x, -10, 10}, {y, -5, 5},
   PlotPoints -> 500,
   Mesh -> False];
```

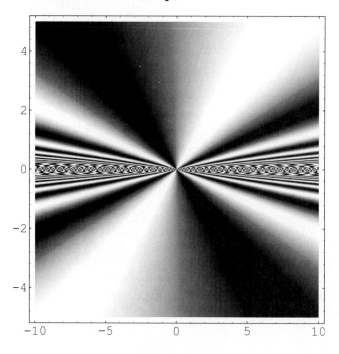

■ Worked Example

Jerry: How would you decide which to choose: **Plot3D**, **ContourPlot**, or **DensityPlot**?

Theo: The best one to use depends mostly on the function you are plotting. **Plot3D** is the first one to try, usually. It gives the most easily interpreted picture. **ContourPlot** allows you to see the shapes of peaks and valleys more accurately. The main advantage of **DensityPlot**, in most cases, is that it is the fastest and most efficient of the three. The example of a 500 by 500 grid we did earlier in this chapter would not be practical as a **Plot3D** or a **ContourPlot** on all but the largest computers. But as a **Density-Plot** it takes less than 15 minutes on a NeXT computer.

Chapter 31
How do I plot a list of values?

The **ListPlot** command plots a list of values in two dimensions:

    ListPlot[{3, 1, 4, 6, 3, 5, 3, 3, 4, 6, 2, 6, 3}];

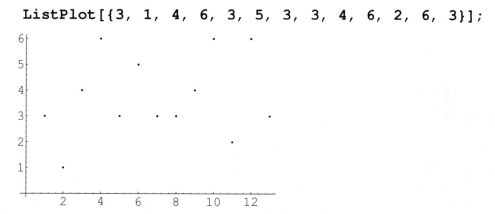

The dots used by **ListPlot** are sometimes too small. They can be increased using the **PlctStyle** option:

    ListPlot[{3, 1, 4, 6, 3, 5, 3, 3, 4, 6, 2, 6, 3},
        PlotStyle -> PointSize[0.02]];

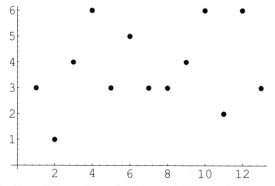

The **PointSize** number, **0.02** in our example, specifies the size of the dots as a fraction of the width of the plot.

The option **PlotJoined -> True** draws a line connecting the points:

```
ListPlot[{3, 1, 4, 6, 3, 5, 3, 3, 4, 6, 2, 6, 3},
              PlotJoined -> True];
```

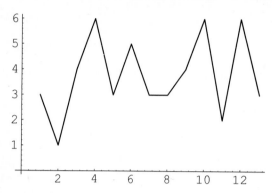

In all these cases the points were drawn with even horizontal spacing.

If you want to specify both x and y values for the points, you can give **ListPlot** a list of pairs of numbers:

```
ListPlot[{{2, 5}, {1, 7}, {2, 9}, {3, 8},
             {4, 9}, {3, 6}, {4, 5}, {0, 0}},
             PlotJoined -> True];
```

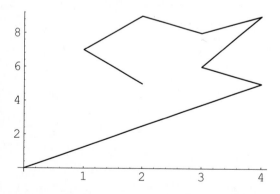

There are, as usual, many options and additional features associated with **ListPlot**. See The *Mathematica* Book for more details.

It is frequently useful to use the **Table** command together with **ListPlot**.
Here is an example:

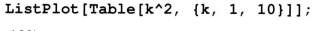

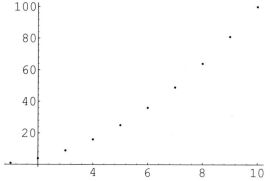

The command **ListPlot3D** works a little differently from **ListPlot**. It
takes a matrix (list of lists) of *z* values:

```
ListPlot3D[{{1, 3, 5},
           {4, 3, 2},
           {2, 3, 4}}];
```

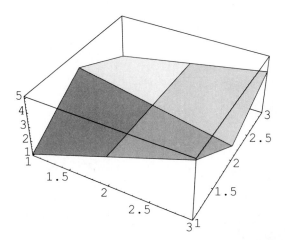

This is analogous to the form of **ListPlot** in which you don't specify *x*
values. The matrix of *z* values is drawn with regularly spaced *x* and *y*
values. There is no way to specify *x* and *y* values manually: You must have
a regular grid. There is also no way to plot points instead of a surface.

(Both of these things can be done using more complicated *Mathematica*
commands, but that is beyond the scope of this book.)

Here is an example made with **Table**:

```
ListPlot3D[Table[Mod[i, j], {i, 1, 20}, {j, 1, 20}]];
```

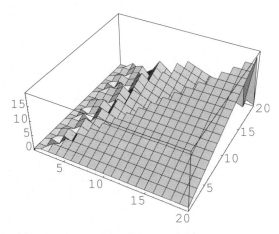

The commands **ListContourPlot** and **ListDensityPlot** work the same
way:

```
ListContourPlot[Table[Mod[i, j],
    {i, 1, 20}, {j, 1, 20}]];
```

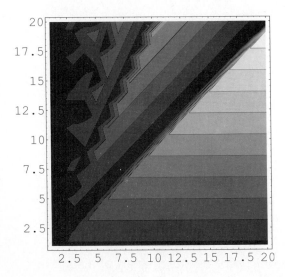

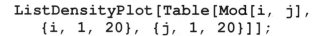

```
ListDensityPlot[Table[Mod[i, j],
   {i, 1, 20}, {j, 1, 20}]];
```

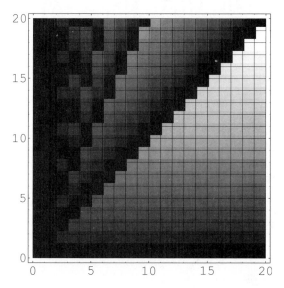

We can define a function to allow us to plot (x, y, z) points in 3D. (You don't need to understand how this function works to use it; type in the definition below, evaluate it, and use it.)

```
pointListPlot3D[list_, options___] :=
   Show[Graphics3D[Map[Point, list]],
     options, Axes -> Automatic]
```

Here is an example using this function:

```
pointListPlot3D[{{1, 2, 2}, {3, 2, 1},
              {2, 1, 1}, {3, 1, 2}}];
```

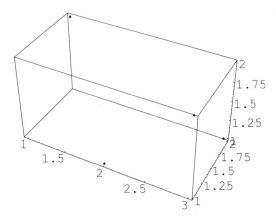

Here is an example made with **Table**:

```
pointListPlot3D[
    Table[{n Cos[n], n Cos[n] Sin[n], n Sin[n]},
      {n, 0, 100, 0.1}]];
```

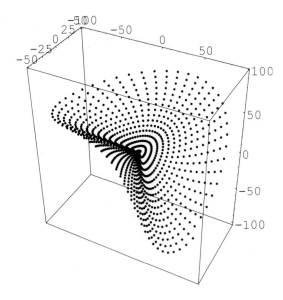

You can use options with this command, just as with built-in plotting commands. For example, you can change the viewpoint:

```
pointListPlot3D[
    Table[{n Cos[n], n Cos[n] Sin[n], n Sin[n]},
        {n, 0, 100, 0.1}],
    ViewPoint->{3.0, 0.0, 0.0}];
```

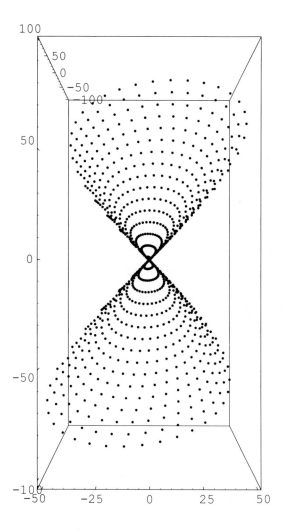

This viewpoint could have been generated with the graphical 3D viewpoint selector, described in Chapter 27, "How do I plot a function in three dimensions?".

Chapter 32
How do I make sounds?

The **Play** command works very much like the **Plot** command. Here is a one-second burst of middle C:

```
Play[Sin[263 2Pi t], {t, 0, 1}];
```

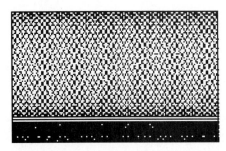

• The first argument is a function that specifies the amplitude waveform, in this case a sine wave that oscillates 263 times per second.

• The second argument is a standard iterator specification, in this case saying that **t** should run from **0** to **1**. (The variable range is always in units of seconds; in this example, we have specified a one-second sound.)

The output shown above is what you will see in a Notebook version of *Mathematica*. It is a rough plot of the waveform. (Don't try to read too much into the pictures associated with sounds; they are mostly placeholders.)

The sound will be played once automatically when the command is executed. In Notebook versions the sound can be replayed at any time by double-clicking on the small, speaker-like icon at the top of the cell bracket of the output cell (the cell bracket is the tall, thin bracket on the right edge of the window).

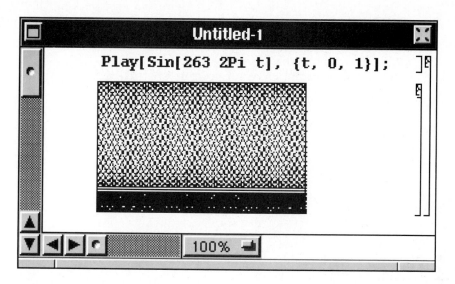

In raw terminal versions it may or may not be possible to replay the sound: Consult your user's manual for information about your specific version.

In *Mathematica* sounds are represented as amplitude waveforms. You can think of an amplitude waveform as a specification of how the speaker cone should move back and forth in time. A rapidly oscillating sine function will produce a pure tone. Most of us have a chance of hearing this tone if it is between about 20 and 20000 cycles per second, depending on our age and the quality of the speakers connected to our computers.

The relationship between a function and what it sounds like is delightful and often surprising. Experimentation is rewarding. The following books may be helpful to people interested in learning more about computer-generated sounds and music:

> • The beginning chapters of *The Technology of Computer Music* by Max V. Matthews (MIT Press, 1969) contain a good introduction to waveforms, samples, and sound.
> • *The Technology of Electronic Music*, by Thomas H. Wells, has a good description of the mathematics of sound production. It is written for musicians.

• *Horns, Strings, and Harmony*, by Arthur Benade, is a good general introduction to acoustics.

Rather than try to explain acoustics, we're going to show a few more examples of sounds. Here is a tone that rises in volume:

```
Play[t Sin[263 2Pi t], {t, 0, 2}];
```

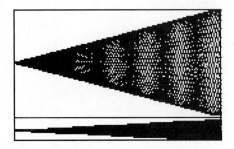

Here is a tone that falls in volume:

```
Play[(2-t) Sin[263 2Pi t], {t, 0, 2}];
```

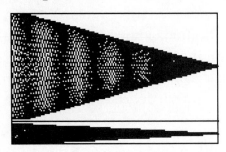

Here is a tone that changes in frequency over time:

```
Play[Sin[263 2Pi t + 2 Sin[5 2Pi t]], {t, 0, 1}];
```

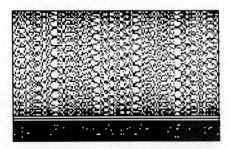

And finally, here is a quite strange sound:

```
Play[Sin[263 2Pi t Sin[5 2Pi t]], {t, 0, 4}];
```

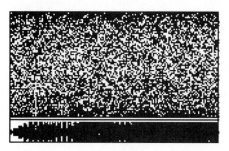

If you want to generate a stereo sound, you can give **Play** a list of two functions as its first argument. This example generates a sound that oscillates from left to right:

```
Play[
    {Sin[2 2Pi t] Sin[263 2Pi t],
     Cos[2 2Pi t] Sin[263 2Pi t]},
    {t, 0, 4}];
```

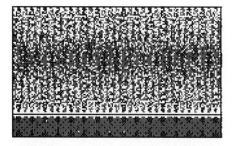

Just as **Play** is analogous to **Plot**, the function **ListPlay** is analogous to **ListPlot**. It takes a list of amplitude values as its first argument. In order to get an audible sound, you need at least several hundred elements in the list.

We can use a **Table** command to generate a list of 10000 random numbers:

```
theList = Table[Random[], {10000}];
```

Now we can play the list. It sounds like noise:

`ListPlay[theList];`

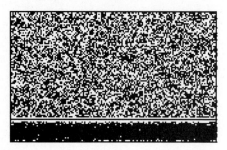

The preceding samples are assumed to be spaced regularly in time, at a
sample rate that depends on the type of computer you are using. You can
find out the value by executing the following command on your
computer:

`Options[ListPlay]`

```
{Epilog -> {}, PlayRange -> Automatic, Prolog -> {},
   SampleDepth -> 8, SampleRate -> 8192,
   DisplayFunction :> $SoundDisplayFunction}
```

This indicates that the default sample rate on our computer is 8192
samples per second.

We have seen how to generate sounds. *Why* we generate them is a little
harder to answer. Sound is a bit like graphics. If you go to your tight-
fisted boss and ask for an expensive new graphics computer so you can
look at pretty pictures of your data, she might well say: "Why do you need
an expensive new graphics computer? Can't you just look at tables of
numbers? There's nothing in the graph that isn't in the table of numbers,
too!"

Your boss is right, of course: A graph is just a different way of presenting a table of numbers. But consider the following table of numbers:

```
theList =
{0.319715, 0.485847, 0.0923159, 0.0098825, 0.385929, 0.178038, 0.341105
 0.0715364, 0.324725, 0.311999, 0.388032, 0.263058, 0.11791, 0.320445,
 0.343071, 0.0754845, 0.130683, 0.424873, 0.279234, 0.037206, 0.07216,
 0.112803, 0.374125, 0.327434, 0.216648, 0.0244873, 0.238622, 0.206607,
 0.437618, 0.379319, 0.415, 0.392528, 0.194673, 0.251138, 0.262301,
 0.28169, 0.425391, 0.0162718, 0.0444506, 0.185095, 0.114933, 0.378389,
 0.171372, 0.45134, 0.395277, 0.339315, 0.0261299, 0.141234, 0.291518,
 0.0446079, 0.0847202, 0.152716, 0.0554939, 0.323003, 0.439467, 0.35632
 0.205486, 0.310317, 0.304329, 0.314771, 0.431105, 0.3075, 0.226201,
 0.45382, 0.21717, 0.0663305, 0.107625, 0.286818, 0.326595, 0.252058,
 0.493203, 0.0588209, 0.421135, 0.310719, 0.149446, 0.316892, 0.370461,
 0.424399, 0.31233, 0.437353, 0.262912, 0.355528, 0.133567, 0.105028,
 0.226203, 0.539964, 0.316752, 0.351406, 0.140764, 0.472047, 0.50166,
 0.350244, 0.445996, 0.421884, 0.418805, 0.533522, 0.749913, 0.721833,
 0.563492, 0.857063, 0.925731, 0.692484, 0.928162, 0.786661, 0.466355,
 0.796613, 0.828478, 0.699389, 0.692961, 0.531652, 0.2786, 0.247609,
 0.575035, 0.185248, 0.287415, 0.329739, 0.428317, 0.27165, 0.0751154,
 0.288455, 0.433856, 0.211975, 0.362165, 0.0665307, 0.240438, 0.0322182
 0.0630494, 0.373264, 0.450873, 0.397439, 0.0888916, 0.051499, 0.270546
 0.351316, 0.102244, 0.448887, 0.196265, 0.176743, 0.00485408, 0.026534
 0.405754, 0.407488, 0.140808, 0.450605, 0.255624, 0.470927, 0.0312255,
 0.204807, 0.486395, 0.466302, 0.393382, 0.406347, 0.0162974, 0.498776,
 0.48806, 0.237831, 0.465167, 0.14923, 0.229618, 0.0469642, 0.0742334,
 0.218719, 0.318047, 0.0478268, 0.326195, 0.105225, 0.0610618, 0.432484
 0.211114, 0.333835, 0.205898, 0.1406, 0.0290034, 0.490678, 0.0952368,
 0.282453, 0.0834089, 0.296256, 0.0182374, 0.122067, 0.392832, 0.198725
 0.462634, 0.0451753, 0.0203656, 0.1584, 0.263841, 0.242207, 0.0865999,
 0.318615, 0.46402, 0.0559252, 0.314072, 0.155495, 0.179808, 0.0758203,
 0.271105, 0.216623, 0.203976, 0.298223, 0.414241, 0.0561329, 0.43637,
 0.0667133, 0.454853, 0.485276, 0.259964, 0.0832396, 0.246328, 0.137695
 0.232986, 0.486746, 0.220911, 0.47477, 0.454641, 0.21976, 0.259378,
 0.366005, 0.1741, 0.299719, 0.271224, 0.239087, 0.260021, 0.359904,
 0.0967571, 0.0157834, 0.494801, 0.281239, 0.167156, 0.0995831, 0.32732
 0.284685, 0.493202, 0.433524, 0.319655, 0.331418, 0.432356, 0.105132,
 0.118675, 0.00205324, 0.447886, 0.226593, 0.453255, 0.167673, 0.404586
 0.0286443, 0.39542, 0.147305, 0.244961, 0.277885, 0.451088};
```

Not very enlightening. We would have to stare at this list for quite a long
time to see what we can see easily in this plot of the same list:

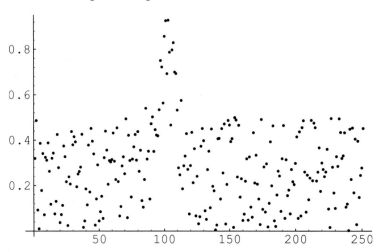

Likewise, consider this list of numbers (abbreviated for space reasons):

```
theList = {
0.00781,  0.00000,  -0.01562,  -0.01562,  -0.03125,  -0.00781,  0.03125,  0.05
0.03906,  -0.03906,  -0.08594,  -0.10156,  -0.10156,  -0.05469,  -0.01562,  0.
0.03906,  0.03125,  0.03906,  0.06250,  0.08594,  0.08594,  0.02344,  -0.00781
-0.00781,  -0.04688,  -0.05469,  -0.03906,  -0.03906,  -0.03906,  -0.07031,  -
0.02344,  0.03125,  0.00781,  -0.04688,  -0.08594,  -0.08594,  -0.10156,  -0.0
-0.03125,  -0.00781,  0.01562,  0.03125,  0.04688,  0.08594,  0.06250,  0.0234
0.00781,  0.00781,  -0.00781,  -0.06250,  -0.09375,  -0.06250,  -0.05469,  -0.
-0.01562,  -0.00781,  0.02344,  -0.00781,  -0.03125,  -0.00781,  0.00781,  -0.
-0.07031,  -0.08594,  -0.04688,  -0.02344,  0.00000,  0.04688,  0.07031,  0.09
0.10938,  0.14062,  0.14844,  0.14062,  0.11719,  0.01562,  -0.07031,  -0.0859
-0.10156,  -0.09375,  -0.03125,  -0.00781,  0.00000,  0.00781,  0.03906,  0.05
0.01562,  -0.03906,  -0.09375,  -0.16406,  -0.15625,  -0.10156,  -0.04688,  0.
0.01562,  -0.00781,  0.01562,  0.05469,  0.11719,  0.09375,  0.00000,  -0.0390
-0.11719,  -0.15625,  -0.11719,  -0.09375,  -0.03906,  -0.03906,  -0.02344,  0
0.10156,  0.10156,  0.07812,  -0.04688,  -0.12500,  -0.17188,  -0.21094,  -0.1
-0.07031,  0.01562,  0.01562,  0.00781,  0.10938,  0.15625,  0.16406,  0.16406
0.13281,  0.03906,  -0.08594,  -0.14062,  -0.09375,  -0.03906,  0.02344,  0.07
```

Also not very enlightening. But if you use **ListPlay** on the complete list:

```
ListPlay[theList];
```

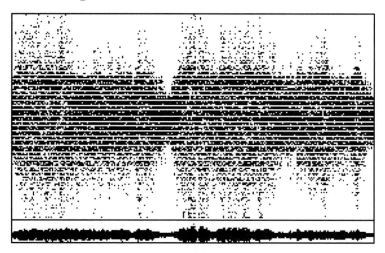

You get a five-second excerpt from the choral section of Beethoven's Ninth Symphony (honestly).

It's rare for a *Mathematica* command to produce a sound as beautiful as the immortal Ninth, but listening to a function can give you new insights into its mathematical properties. It's also a lot of fun.

Chapter 33
How do I make animations?

Making animations is one of the great pleasures of *Mathematica*. Many a pleasant Sunday afternoon can be spent in front of the screen making *Mathematica* animations.

Mathematica animations are much like Hollywood animations: They are a sequence of pictures that, when displayed in rapid succession, appear to move. (If you aren't familar with the graphics commands in *Mathematica*, you might want to read some of the relevant chapters in this book before reading this chapter.)

In Notebook front end versions of *Mathematica*, any sequence of graphics cells can be animated using the Animate Selected Graphics command in the Graph menu. For example, the following command will generate a sequence of six graphics, each slightly different from the others:

```
Do[
    Plot[Sin[n x], {x, 0, 2Pi}],
    {n, 1, 2, 0.2}
];
```

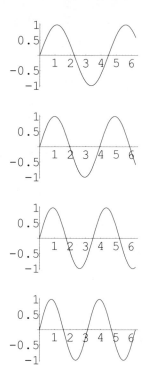

(**Do** is a general-purpose iteration command: This example says to repeat the **Plot** command six times, with values of **n** ranging from **1** to **2** in steps of **0.2**.)

To see these graphics animated, double-click on one of the pictures (any one will do). The cell group containing the pictures will be selected and the animation started, automatically.

If you are using a raw terminal (UNIX or MS-DOS) version, you can't make animations with **Do**. You have to load the standard package Animation.m (included in all copies of *Mathematica* Version 2). You can load it with the following command:

    Needs["Graphics `Animation`"];

(Note that the two single quotes used here are "back quotes" usually found on the same key with ~. They are not the single quotes found on the double-quote key.)

The package defines the command **Animate**, which takes the same arguments as **Do**, but works to make an animation in any version of *Mathematica*. For example, we can make the same animation as above using **Animate** instead of **Do**:

```
Animate[
    Plot[Sin[n x], {x, 0, 2Pi}],
    {n, 1, 2, 0.2}
]
```

We didn't include the pictures because they are exactly the same as before.

From now on we'll use **Animate** because it works in any version of *Mathematica*. We'll show the frames of the animations in a two-dimensional layout, to save space. When you make these animations in your own copy of
Mathematica, they will not be displayed in this form.

There are a number of issues that we did not need to deal with in our first,
fairly simple animation. The most important is the plot range. Consider
this slight variation:

```
Animate[
    Plot[Sin[n x], {x, 0, 2Pi}],
    {n, 0, 1, 0.2}
];
```

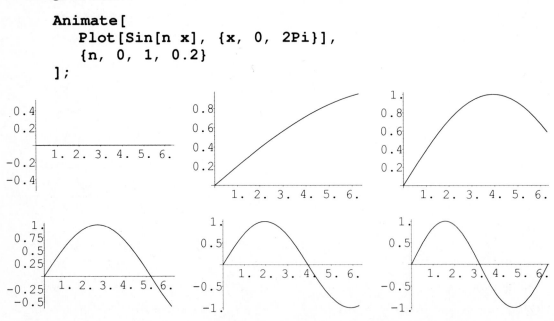

In this example, *Mathematica* automatically chose a different *y* range for each of the first few plots. This makes the axes jump around. It is almost always necessary to specify a fixed plot range when making animations. The **PlotRange** option allows us to do so:

```
Animate[
    Plot[Sin[n x], {x, 0, 2Pi}, PlotRange->{-1, 1}],
    {n, 0, 1, 0.2}
];
```

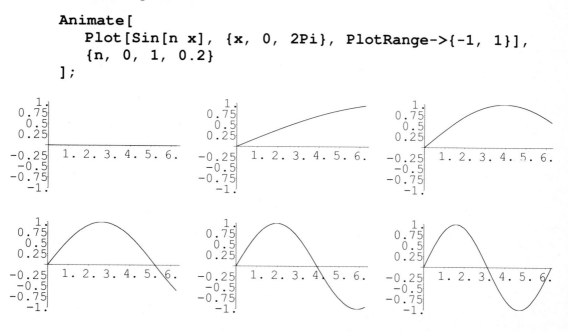

For more details of how to specify plot ranges, see Chapter 22, "How do I plot a function in two dimensions?".

Following are some edifying animations. They show how to use the animation parameter to move a parabola around in different ways:

```
Animate[Plot[a x^2, {x, -3, 3},
        PlotRange -> {{-3, 3}, {-25, 25}}],
    {a, -4, 4, 0.25}];

Animate[Plot[x^2 + a, {x, -3, 3},
        PlotRange -> {{-3, 3}, {-25, 25}}],
    {a, -4, 4, 0.25}];

Animate[Plot[(x - a)^2, {x, -12, 12},
        PlotRange -> {{-3, 3}, {0, 64}}],
    {a, -4, 4, 0.25}];
```

We can make 3D animations in the same way, using **Plot3D** instead of
Plot. (Warning: 3D animations can take a long time to generate and use a
lot of memory!)

```
Animate[
    Plot3D[Sin[n x] Sin[n y], {x,0,2Pi}, {y,0,2Pi},
          PlotRange -> {-1, 1}],
    {n, 1, 2, 0.1}
];
```

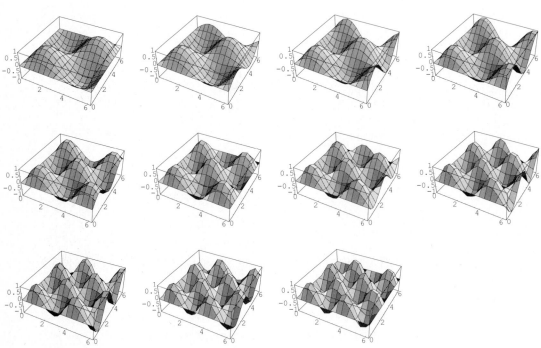

In fact, we can make animations with any *Mathematica* graphics command.
For example, the following is a contour plot animation. (It is just as easy to
make animations using the various other graphics commands.)

```
Animate[
   ContourPlot[Sin[x^2 + y^2] Cos[(x - n)^2 + y^2],
      {x, -2, 2}, {y, -2, 2},
      PlotRange -> {-1, 1}],
   {n, -2, 2, 0.2}
];
```

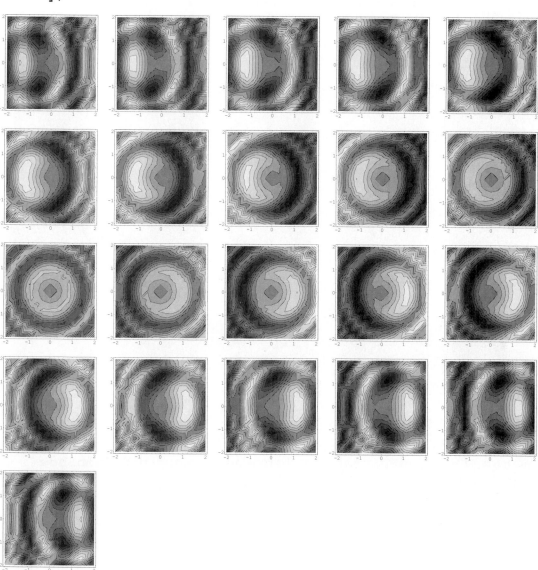

We can also make animations in which we change options of the plotting
commands instead of changing the function being plotted. For example, in
this animation we change the range over which the function is plotted:

```
Animate[
    Plot3D[Sin[x y], {x, -n, n}, {y, -n, n}],
    {n, 1, 3, 0.2}
];
```

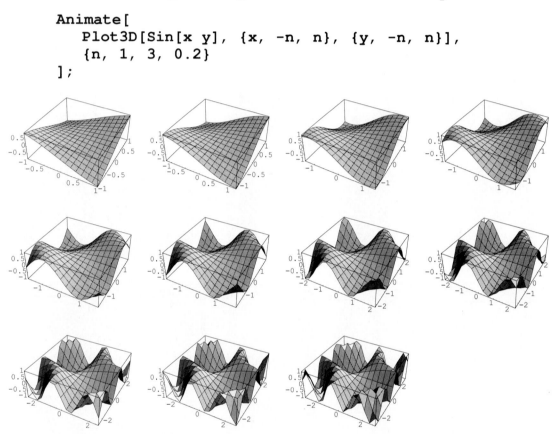

A particularly common variation of this is to change the viewpoint, to
make a surface appear to rotate. Although you could do this using **Animate** and the **ViewPoint** option, there is a special function, **SpinShow**
(defined in Animation.m), that does it for you.

To use **SpinShow**, first generate the surface you want to rotate. (It's important to use the option **Axes->None**, because if there are any axes in the plot, the animation will not come out right.)

```
Plot3D[Sin[x y], {x, 0, 3}, {y, 0, 3},
    Axes -> None];
```

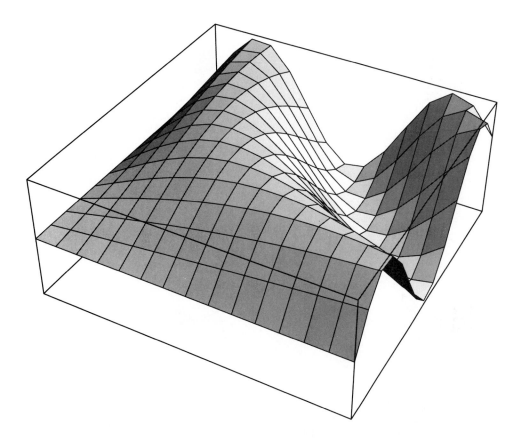

Then use **SpinShow** on the result (**%** means the result of the last evaluation):

```
SpinShow[%];
```

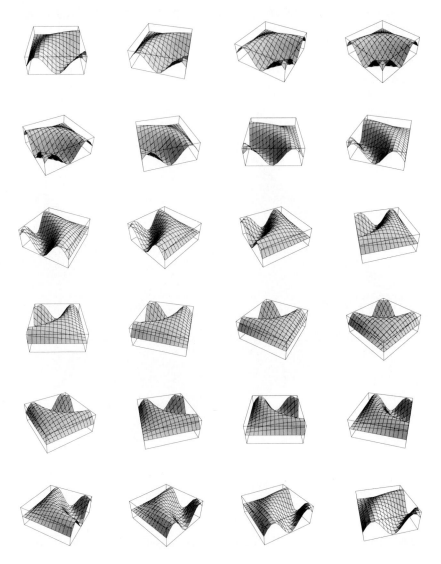

There are several options to **SpinShow** that specify how many steps to generate, over what range to rotate the surface, etc. They are described in the package documentation that came with your copy of *Mathematica*.

For further examples of peculiar animations, see our earlier book, *Exploring Mathematics with Mathematica*.

Chapter 34
How do I use *Mathematica* as a word processor?

Just start typing.

If you are using a raw terminal version of *Mathematica*, you can skip this chapter; everything in it applies only to Notebook front ends.

The *Mathematica* Notebook interface is, in many ways, a word processor with a few extra features. When you open a new *Mathematica* Notebook window, you see an empty space with a horizontal line near the top (this line is called the *cell insertion point*). Here is what an empty window looks like on a NeXT computer:

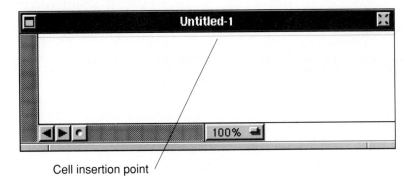

Cell insertion point

Here is the same window on a Macintosh:

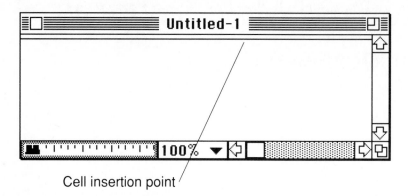

Cell insertion point

From now on, we'll show only NeXT versions. Except for the items in the window border, everything would look almost identical on any other Notebook version.

As soon as you start typing, a new "cell" is created to hold what you type. The cell is shown by a bracket on the right side of the window. If you type several lines (using the Return key to begin new lines) the cell bracket will grow to enclose everything you type. Here is what a two-line cell looks like:

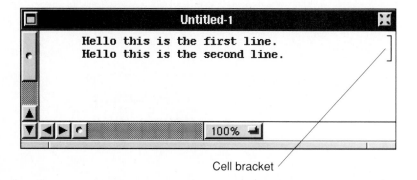

Cell bracket

The text in a cell can be manipulated in much the same way as you manipulate text in any other word processor. You can use the mouse and the Cut, Copy, Paste, and Delete (or Clear) commands in the normal way. (The versions of *Mathematica* for Macintosh, NeXT, and MS Windows each conform to the local customs and traditions of their respective hosts.)

If you click the mouse just below the bottom of your cell, you will get a horizontal line across the width of the window. This is the cell insertion point again:

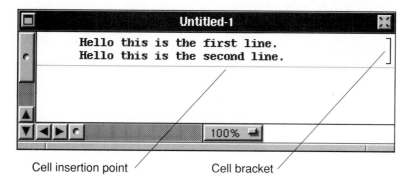

Cell insertion point   Cell bracket

If you start typing, a new cell will be created below the first one. You can tell the difference between one large cell and two smaller cells by the brackets on the right hand side:

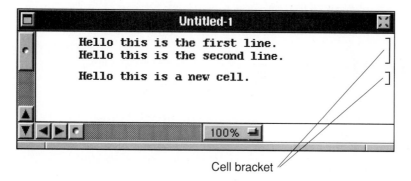

Cell bracket

You can select and manipulate cells in much the same way as you select and manipulate characters in text:

- To select a cell, click on its cell bracket.

- To place the cell insertion point, click between two cells, or above or below the first or last cells.

- To select more than one cell, click on one cell bracket and then drag over the others.

• To cut, copy, or delete cells, select them and then use the appropriate menu command.

• To insert cells you have copied, place the cell insertion point and then use the Paste command.

Every cell has a *cell style* that determines the default attributes of that cell. When you create a new cell by typing, it is, by default, in the Input cell style, which is normally Courier font, boldface, 12-point type.

When you evaluate an expression, the output is placed in a new cell with the Output cell style. This style is similar to Input, except that it is not boldface. The combination of these two styles gives the typical bold/non-bold look of a calculation session:

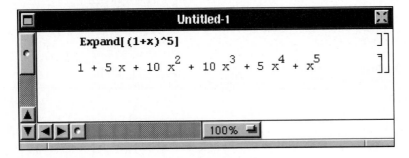

If you use *Mathematica* only as a calculator, these are the only two styles you will typically see in the Notebooks that you create. By using a few other styles, though, you can turn your Notebooks into complete documents.

You may notice that there are two cell brackets and a third larger one that encloses them. This enclosing bracket is called a *group bracket* and is discussed in Chapter 35, "How do I use *Mathematica* as an outliner?".

There are several ways to change the cell style of a cell. The easiest is to choose the Show Ruler command in the Style menu (Macintosh) or Format menu (NeXT). This will put the margins ruler at the top of the window:

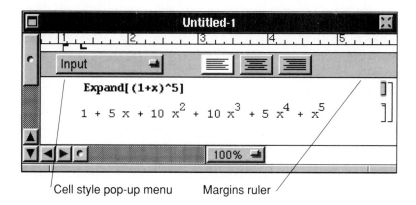

Cell style pop-up menu   Margins ruler

Click above the first cell to place the cell insertion point, and then choose Text from the cell style pop-up menu:

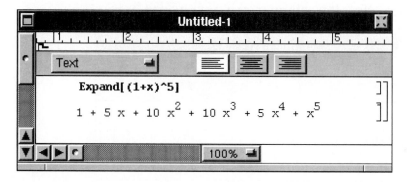

Now start typing:

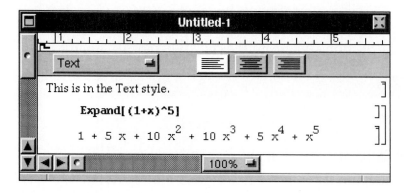

The new cell is in the Text style. (Choosing a cell style while the selection is a cell insertion point is like choosing a font while the selection is a text insertion point—it affects the style of the next cell created there.)

This style has a nicer-looking (proportional spaced) font, is aligned to the left of input and output, and is set up so lines longer than one page width are automatically wrapped. (Each cell style is a collection of many individual attributes and settings. These are described in more detail in the front end user's manual that came with your copy of *Mathematica*. In this book we're just going to talk about how to use styles, not how to redefine them.)

We might want to make the first cell in this example into a section heading. To do this, we first select the cell by clicking on its cell bracket:

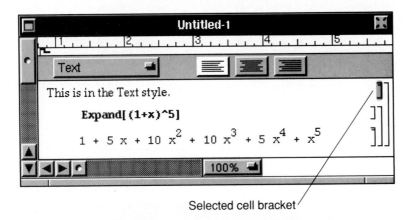

Selected cell bracket

Then we choose the Section style from the cell style pop-up menu:

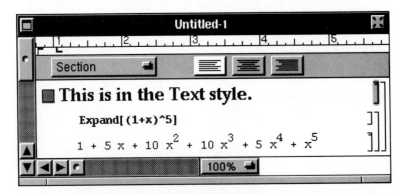

Of course, the text "This is in the Text style." is wrong now!

The Section heading style includes larger, bold text and a square dingbat. As we mentioned before, these attributes can all be redefined using techniques described in the user's manual that came with your copy of *Mathematica*.

A very useful shortcut to know is that each style has a command-key equivalent. Following are the most useful predefined styles along with their command keys:

Title style, Command-1

Subtitle style, Command-2

Subsubtitle style, Command-3

■ Section style, Command-4

■ Subsection style, Command-5

□ Subsubsection style, Command-6

Text style, Command-7

Small Text style, Command-8

`Input style, Command-9`

The margins ruler can be used to change some of the attributes of cells. We've already seen how to use the cell style pop-up menu to change the style of cells. The three buttons to the right of the pop-up menu are used to change the alignment of the text in the selected cells. For example, to center align the Section heading in the last example, select the first cell and click the center button:

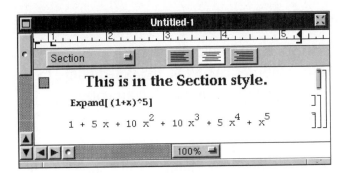

The three small markers in the ruler section can be used to change the left
and right margins of the cell and the left indent of the cell names
(`In[]`/`Out[]` labels).

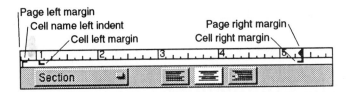

The page left and right margins can't be adjusted using this ruler (they can
be changed only by using the Printing Options dialog box, described in
the user's manual that came with your copy of *Mathematica*).

To change a margin setting, select the cells you want to affect and then
click and drag one of the margin indicators. For example, we could
crunch the section heading into a narrow band:

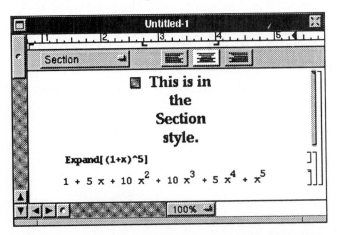

■ Worked Example

Let us imagine that we want to write a book about *Mathematica* called *The Beginner's Guide to Mathematica*. We want to do it entirely in *Mathematica*, of course. We'll do a short chapter on factoring and expanding polynomials.

First we need to think of a few good examples of factoring and expanding. We can quickly type these in, using *Mathematica* like a calculator:

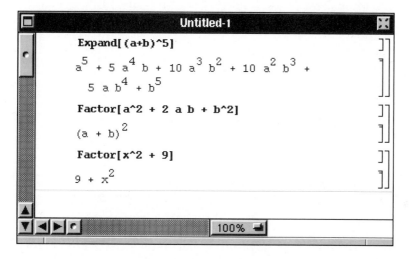

Let's add a title. We move the mouse to the space between the top of the first cell and the top of the window (the pointer will change into a horizontal bar when we are in the right place), and then click. A horizontal bar (the cell insertion point) appears across the whole width of the window. We type Command-1 (one), or Alt-1 on a DOS computer, to choose the Title style. Then we type in our title. A new cell in the Title style will be created when we type the first character.

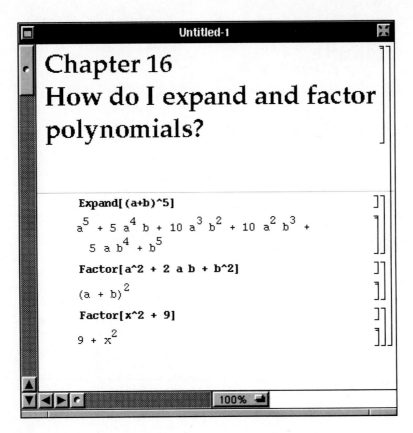

Ignore for now the growing number of large, enclosing brackets on the right side. They are described in Chapter 35, "How do I use *Mathematica* as an outliner?".

Since the Title cell style specifies bold text, the title is bold. We want only the "Chapter 16" to be bold, so we select the rest of the title with the mouse and choose Unbold from the Font submenu of the Format menu (NeXT) or Bold from the Face submenu of the Style menu (Macintosh):

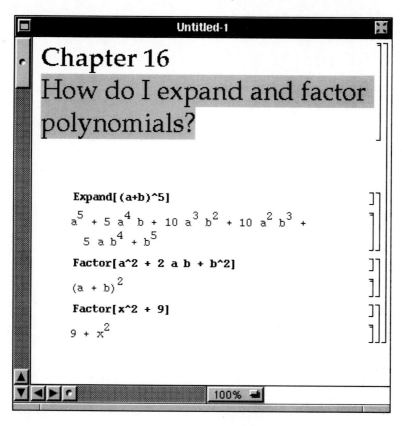

Next we click between the bottom of the Title cell and the top of the first example cell, to get another cell insertion point. This time we use Command-7 to get the Text style, and then type some text. We can add more Text cells in the same way, giving this result:

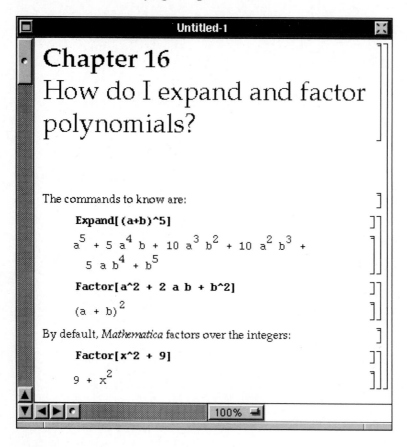

The word *Mathematica* is put in italics automatically whenever it is typed.

Now we have the beginnings of a chapter. If you want to see the rest, turn to Chapter 17, "How do I manipulate polynomials?", in this book. Yes, this whole book was printed directly from *Mathematica*. The words you are reading right now are in a text cell created in exactly the way described here.

Chapter 35
How do I use *Mathematica* as an outliner?

Before reading this chapter, you should read Chapter 34, "How do I use *Mathematica* as a word processor?", which describes cells and cell styles. You need to understand cells before reading this chapter.

In Chapter 34 we mentioned the large, enclosing brackets (called group brackets) that appear in some of the examples, such as this one:

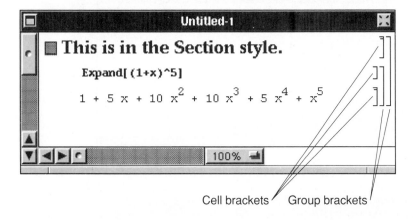

Cell brackets   Group brackets

These group brackets are the heart of the *Mathematica* outlining system. If you double-click a group bracket, all the cells in the group are collapsed, leaving only the first cell (called the *head cell*) visible. For example, if you double-click the group bracket enclosing the bottom two cells, the result looks like this:

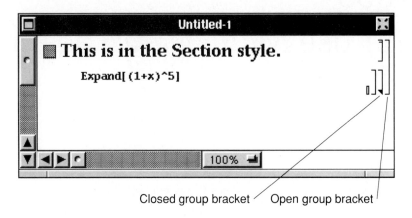

Closed group bracket   Open group bracket

If you double-click the outermost (right-most) group bracket, the result
looks like this:

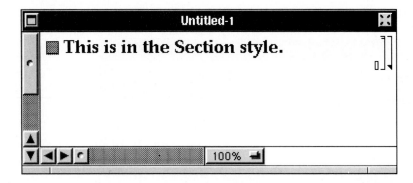

Double-clicking the closed group bracket opens it up again:

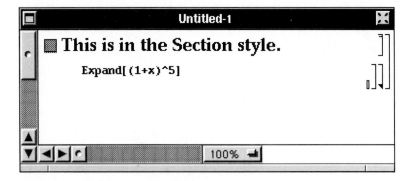

Notice that the inner group is still closed: Each group remains open or
closed individually, regardless of groups enclosing them.

The small box that appears to the left of the head cell's bracket when its group is closed is called the *closed group box*. Its width is proportional to the number of hidden cells in the group, and it is used to show selections of hidden cells.

To see the usefulness of groups, consider the following Notebook (you can use the techniques discussed in Chapter 34, "How do I use *Mathematica* as a word processor?", to create this Notebook):

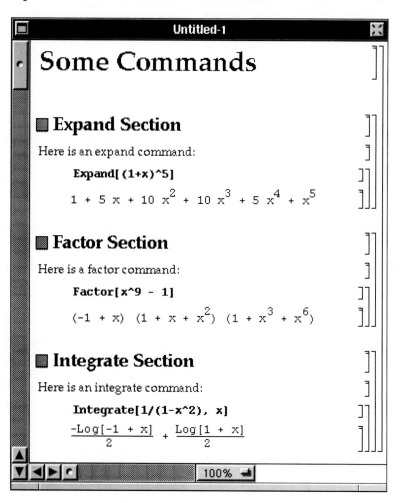

As long as all the cells are in the appropriate cell style (title in the Title style, section headings in the Section style, commentary cells in the Text style, etc.), the cells will automatically be grouped as shown.

Now if we double-click each of the group brackets that enclose a section, we get this:

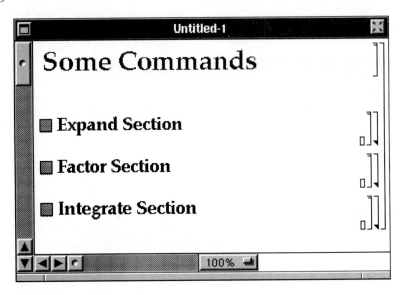

The window doesn't actually get smaller, we're just showing it that way to save space.

If these sections were longer than in this example, this form would allow you to see much more of the Notebook at once. For example, if you wanted to see what was in the Factor Section, you could double-click the closed group bracket for that section and see this:

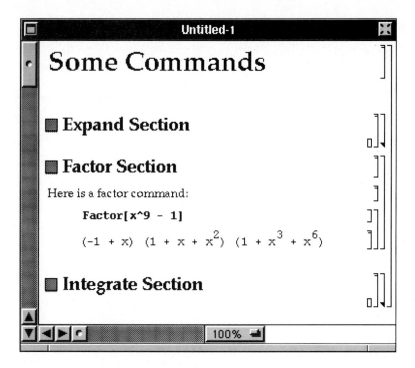

By adding more sections, or subsections within sections (using the Subsection or Subsubsection cell styles), you can create a whole structured document and get to anywhere in it quickly.

Cell groupings are ordinarily created automatically, based on the cell styles of the cells in the Notebook. For example, Section headings begin a group that encloses everything up to the next Section. Subsection headings enclose everything up to the next Section or Subsection, etc. Titles enclose everything up to the next Title.

Sometimes you might want to override the default groups and make your own. There are two ways to do this: changing the automatic grouping behavior of cells, or turning off the automatic grouping altogether.

Each cell style is a collection of individual attributes (font, size, dingbat, etc.). One of these attributes is the cell's automatic grouping behavior. For example, Section, Subsection, and Subsubsection style cells have the attribute Group Like Section. By changing this attribute, you can make a cell enclose more or fewer of the cells below it. (For more details about how to change this attribute, see the user's manual that came with your version of *Mathematica*. Editing styles are quite different between different versions of *Mathematica* and are not discussed in this book.)

If you can't do what you want by changing cell attributes, you can turn off automatic grouping. Choose the Automatic Grouping command in the Cell menu (if automatic grouping is enabled, the command will be checked (Macintosh) or boldface (NeXT), and will become unchecked or unbold when you choose it). Automatic grouping is now disabled for the current Notebook (other Notebooks are not affected, since this setting is remembered on a per-Notebook basis).

Any existing groups will remain in the Notebook, but if you add new cells they will not be grouped in with existing ones. You can use the Group Cells and Ungroup Cells commands in the Cell menu to add and remove groups manually.

To remove a group, select the whole group by clicking on the group bracket that encloses it and then choose Ungroup Cells. To group a range of cells together, select all of them and then choose Group Cells. To add a cell to the bottom of a group, select the last cell in the group and the cell you want to add and then choose Group Cells.

Chapter 36
How do I do statistics?

There are dozens of statistics programs available for almost all brands of computers. They range from simple, inexpensive, programs that students can use to draw shaky conclusions from their experiments, to sophisticated, expensive, programs that professional sociologists do use to draw shaky conclusions from *their* experiments.

How does *Mathematica* compare to these programs as a statistical analysis tool? It can carry out most of the statistical analyses that the better special-purpose programs can, and it can draw most of the same plots that they can. It can read files of data in almost any text format (many other programs require the data to be in one of a small number of possible formats).

On the other hand, *Mathematica* does not have a spreadsheet-like interface for entering data. Lists of data have to be entered as *Mathematica* lists (unless the data is stored in a file). *Mathematica* is relatively inefficient when dealing with very large data sets (e.g., 10,000 or more data points), so it will take more time and memory to carry out analyses than will a special-purpose program (on the other hand, many special purpose programs are unable to handle such large datasets at all). *Mathematica* also requires somewhat more learning to use for the first time. However, some of the more sophisticated special-purpose programs are even harder to use.

Perhaps the biggest advantage of using *Mathematica* to do your statistics is that you always have the whole of *Mathematica* available, not just the statistical portions. If you need to solve an equation on the side, you can. *Mathematica* is also able to carry out a variety of symbolic statistical analyses that data-based numerical programs can't approach.

Having established why you might want to use *Mathematica* to do statistics, how does it work? First, to do any statistics you have to load the standard statistics package (included in all versions of *Mathematica* Version 2). You can load the package with the following command:

```
Needs["Statistics`Master`"]
```

(Note that the two single quotes used here are "back quotes" usually found on the same key with ~. They are *not* the single quotes found on the double-quote key.)

Loading this package makes *Mathematica*'s approximately 185 standard statistical functions available. Obviously we can't describe all of them here (they are all described in the *Guide to Standard Mathematica Packages* that comes with each copy of *Mathematica* Version 2).

We will first discuss descriptive statistics. To do this, we need some data. We can assign a list of 20 not completely random numbers to the variable **theData**:

```
theData = {1.6597, 2.8722, 3.8955, 4.2325, 5.7835,
    6.4807, 7.1861, 8.6568, 9.6286, 10.7319, 10.6251,
    9.2095, 8.4716, 7.8621, 6.2796, 5.6767, 4.8754,
    3.9759, 2.3209, 1.8559};
```

The following examples are given without further discussion. The function names correspond to the traditional names used in statistics (demonstrating once again the value of using fully spelled-out names):

```
Mean[theData]
```
6.11401

```
Median[theData]
```
6.03155

```
GeometricMean[theData]
```
5.34876

HarmonicMean[theData]

4.5124

RootMeanSquare[theData]

6.72815

StandardDeviation[theData]

2.88132

Variance[theData]

8.30199

Skewness[theData]

0.0332837

Kurtosis[theData]

1.66604

There are also three functions that give you collections of these (and other) measures:

LocationReport[theData]

{Mean -> 6.11401, HarmonicMean -> 4.5124,
  Median -> 6.03155}

DispersionReport[theData]

{Variance -> 8.30199,
  StandardDeviation -> 2.88132,
  SampleRange -> 9.0722, MeanDeviation -> 2.39919,
  MedianDeviation -> 2.28805,
  QuartileDeviation -> 2.31425}

ShapeReport[theData]

{Skewness -> 0.0332837,
  QuartileSkewness -> 0.0943718,
  KurtosisExcess -> -1.33396}

Confidence intervals of several sorts can be computed. For example, here is the 95% confidence interval for the mean:

```
MeanCI[theData]
```
```
{4.73048, 7.49754}
```

If you want a difference confidence level, you can use the following form:

```
MeanCI[theData, ConfidenceLevel -> 0.75]
```
```
{5.32963, 6.89839}
```

There are quite a few more measures available: we've shown just a few.

Mathematica can manipulate several continuous and discrete distributions. For example, here is the "normal" distribution with a mean (center) of 6.11 and a standard deviation of 2.88:

```
NormalDistribution[6.11, 2.88]
```
```
NormalDistribution[6.11, 2.88]
```

This object does not, in itself, do anything; it is meaningful only in combination with other statistical functions. For example, we can ask for the mean of this distribution:

```
Mean[NormalDistribution[6.11, 2.88]]
```
```
6.11
```

As expected, the mean is the same as what we specified. The kurtosis is somewhat less trivial:

```
Kurtosis[NormalDistribution[6.11, 2.88]]
```
```
3
```

If we want to make a picture or table of the distribution, we have to get the actual function that describes the probability. This is done with the **PDF** function (which stands for **P**robability **D**istribution **F**unction):

```
normalFunction =
        PDF[NormalDistribution[6.11, 2.88], x]
```

$$\frac{0.347222}{E^{0.0602816\ (-6.11\ +\ x)^{2}}\ \text{Sqrt}[2\ \text{Pi}]}$$

- The first argument is the description of the distribution.
- The second argument is the variable to write the function in terms of.

We can plot this function:

```
Plot[normalFunction, {x, 0, 12}];
```

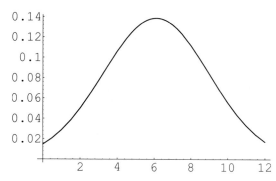

Or we can make a table of values:

```
Table[N[normalFunction], {x, 0, 12, 0.5}]
```

```
{0.0145936, 0.0207768, 0.0287014, 0.0384714,
  0.050036, 0.0631448, 0.0773218, 0.0918707,
  0.105916, 0.118483, 0.128606, 0.135449,
  0.138421, 0.137257, 0.132063, 0.123292,
  0.111686, 0.0981691, 0.0837259, 0.0692875,
  0.0556365, 0.0433485, 0.0327717, 0.02404,
  0.0171111}
```

There are a couple of dozen other distributions available.

Several common statistical plots and charts can be made. We must first load another package, using the following command:

Needs["Graphics`Graphics`"]

(Note that the two single quotes used here are "back quotes" usually found on the same key with ~. They are *not* the single quotes found on the double-quote key.)

Now we can make the following plots of our data (the labels in these plots are the index numbers of each data point within the list of data):

BarChart[theData];

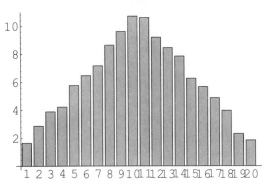

PieChart[theData];

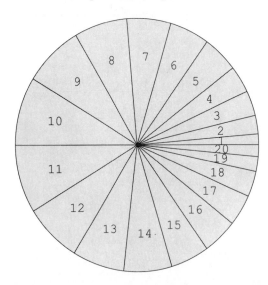

TextListPlot[theData];

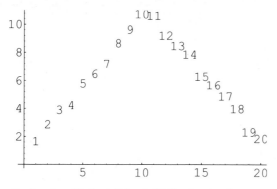

LabeledListPlot[theData];

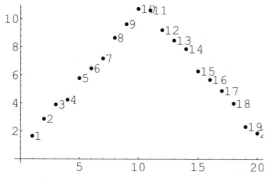

As with other *Mathematica* graphics commands, there are countless options that change the details of the plots. These are all described in the *Guide to Standard Packages*.

Chapter 37
How do I fit a curve to data?

Here is the population of the earth over the last 10 decades, starting in 1900. The data is given as a list of pairs; the first element in each pair is the year since 1900, and the second element is the population in billions:

```
population = {
    {00, 1.59},
    {10, 1.70},
    {20, 1.81},
    {30, 2.02},
    {40, 2.25},
    {50, 2.59},
    {60, 3.01},
    {70, 3.61},
    {80, 4.48},
    {90, 5.33}};
```

We can make a plot of this data using **ListPlot**, which is explained in more detail in Chapter 31, "How do I plot a list of values?":

```
dataPlot = ListPlot[population, PlotJoined -> True];
```

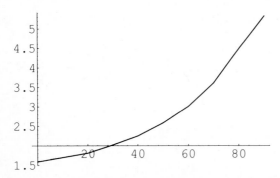

We might want to find a function that approximates this curve. For example, the following command will find the best-fitting third order polynomial:

```
fitFunction = Fit[population, {1, x, x^2, x^3}, x]
```

$$1.59155 + 0.0101523\ x - 4.02098\ 10^{-6}\ x^2 +$$
$$3.96076\ 10^{-6}\ x^3$$

- The first argument is the data to fit.
- The second argument is a list of functions to fit.
- The third argument names the independent variable.

The second argument to **Fit** is a list of functions that will be combined linearly to form the fit function. In the example above, the listed functions are combined like this:

```
a 1 + b x + c x^2 + d x^3
```

$$a + b\ x + c\ x^2 + d\ x^3$$

The job of **Fit** is to choose the values of **a**, **b**, **c**, and **d** to form the best possible fit. (This is called *linear regression* because the coefficients being fit are all linearly related to the fit function. Non-linear regression is much more complicated and will not be discussed here.)

Having found a fit function, we can plot it. **Plot** is discussed in more detail in Chapter 22, "How do I plot a function in two dimensions?":

```
fitPlot = Plot[fitFunction, {x, 0, 100},
          PlotStyle -> Dashing[{0.01}]];
```

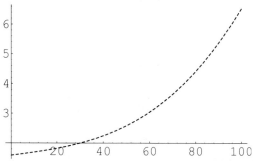

To see how good the fit is, we can show both plots together:

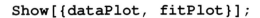

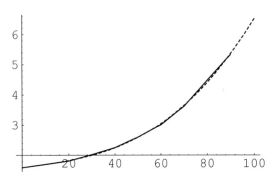

Notice that we have plotted the fit function one decade beyond the end of the data. This illustrates the most common use of curve fitting, called *extrapolation*. It also illustrates the danger of extrapolating beyond the reasonable range of validity: This curve predicts a population of about 6.6 billion in the year 2000, compared to current best estimates of 6.2 billion.

In the example above we fit to a polynomial. Polynomials are commonly used when you have no idea what the data *should* look like: They are generic functions that work anywhere. In this case, however, we know that populations grow more or less exponentially, so we might want to fit to a function of the form:

$$a\ E^{b\ x}$$

$$a\ E^{b\ x}$$

Here **a** and **b** are constants to be determined by **Fit**. Unfortunately, as discussed above, **Fit** works only when the constants are linear. In this example, **b** is in a non-linear position.

Fortunately, we can use a trick: We can fit the log of this function to the log of the data. If we take the log of the function, we get:

$$\texttt{Log[a] + b x}$$

$$b\ x\ +\ \texttt{Log[a]}$$

Now **a** is nonlinearly related to the function, but we can make up a new constant, **loga**, which is linear:

```
loga + b x
```
```
loga + b x
```

If we fit this function to the log of the data, we will get the answer we want.

We want a new table, similar to **population**, but with the **Log** of the second element of each data pair. There are several ways to do this. The following is not the most efficient but is probably the least confusing.

First we define a function, **logOfSecondElement**, which, when applied to a list of two elements, returns a list in which the second element has been replaced by its **Log**:

```
logOfSecondElement[{x_, y_}] := {x, Log[y]}
```

See Chapter 9, "How do I define constants and functions?", and Chapter 40, "How do I use patterns?", for more information on defining functions.

Next we apply (map) this function to each element in the **population** list:

```
logPopulation = Map[logOfSecondElement, population]
```
```
{{0, 0.463734}, {10, 0.530628}, {20, 0.593327},
 {30, 0.703098}, {40, 0.81093}, {50, 0.951658},
 {60, 1.10194}, {70, 1.28371}, {80, 1.49962},
 {90, 1.67335}}
```

Now we can fit one constant plus a second constant times **x** to this new data:

```
Fit[logPopulation, {1, x}, x]
```
```
0.34869 + 0.0136113 x
```

So our constant **loga** is 0.34869, and our constant **b** is 0.0136113. Translating back into the original form of the function, we get:

```
fitFunction2 = E^0.34869 E^(0.0136113 x)
```
$$1.41721 \; E^{0.0136113 \; x}$$

In terms of our original equation, the constant **a** is 1.41721.

We can plot this function:

```
fitPlot2 = Plot[fitFunction2, {x, 0, 100},
          PlotStyle -> Dashing[{0.01}]];
```

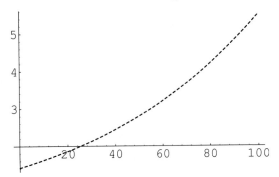

We can combine it with the data:

```
Show[{dataPlot, fitPlot2}];
```

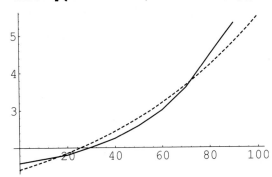

We thereby demonstrate that population growth is not, in fact, purely exponential.

Sadly, a great deal of curve fitting is done without sufficient thought. It's like statistics: A little knowledge can get you into a lot of trouble. Readers are encouraged *not* to use the **Fit** function unless they are qualified to do so by at least two semesters of college statistics, or three books.

Chapter 38
How do I program in *Mathematica*?

Programming in *Mathematica* is a deep subject, but you can do a lot of very useful things without having to learn an unreasonable amount of information. The advanced reader is advised to consult The *Mathematica* Book as well as Roman Maeder's book, *Programming In Mathematica*, second edition (Addison-Wesley, 1991).

This chapter covers traditional procedural programming. Chapter 40, "How do I use patterns?", examines pattern-based programming.

We start with the most basic operation, defining a function:

```
f[n_]  := Expand[(a+b)^n]
```

Here is what this function does:

```
f[2]
```

$$a^2 + 2 \ a \ b + b^2$$

```
f[3]
```

$$a^3 + 3 \ a^2 \ b + 3 \ a \ b^2 + b^3$$

For the purposes of this chapter, we can think of the left hand side of the function definition as an idiomatic form not to be analyzed further. Just think of **f[n_]** as "the function **f** with one argument, named **n**". The definition **f[n_, m_]** is a function of two arguments, named **n** and **m**.

The := means "delayed assignment". The "delayed" part is important here. It means that the right-hand side is not evaluated when we *define* the function, but only when we *use* it. If the right-hand side were evaluated when the function was defined, the **Expand** function would attempt to expand the expression **(a+b)^n**, with **n** not having any specific numerical value. Here is what **Expand** would do:

```
Expand[(a+b)^n]
```

$$(a + b)^n$$

The **Expand** function returned the expression unchanged. So if the function were stored with the right-hand side already evaluated, it would be equivalent to this definition:

```
f[n_] := (a+b)^n
```

This version does not expand anything and is not what we want.

There are cases in which you *do* want to evaluate the right-hand side of an expression when you make the definition, not when you use it. Here is an example:

```
nSin = N[Sin[2]];
```

The = means "non-delayed assignment". In this case we want to evaluate the right-hand side only once, when the definition is made, so we store the numerical value and can access it rapidly without having to recompute the **Sin** each time.

It's usually the case that if you have an _ on the left-hand side of the definition, then you want to use delayed assignment (:=). Otherwise you want to use immediate assignment (=). This is not a hard and fast rule, but it is a useful rule of thumb.

You can define many useful functions just by combining the technique described above with a few built-in *Mathematica* functions. For example, here is a definition of a function that returns the average of a list of numbers:

```
average[list_] := Apply[Plus, list] / Length[list]
```

The expression **Apply[Plus, list]** means apply the **Plus** function
(addition) to all the elements of the list **list**. This has the effect of adding
together all the elements of the list. Dividing by the length of (number of
elements in) **list** gives the average. Here's what the function does:

```
average[{1, 5, 2, 3, 4}]
```
   3

More complicated functions may require the use of local variables. To
avoid possible name conflicts with global variables, it is best to use the
Module function. Here is an example, a function that generates a list of a
specified number of random numbers, prints some facts about the list, and
then returns the list as its value:

```
randomStatistics[n_] := Module[
    {data},

    data = Table[Random[], {n}];

    Print["Maximum = ", Max[data]];
    Print["Minimum = ", Min[data]];
    Print["Average = ", average[data]];

    data
]
```

• The first argument to **Module**, **{data}**, is a list of local variables to be
used inside the **Module**.

• The second argument to **Module** is the body of the function. The value of
the last expression in the body (**data**) is returned as the value of the
Module function, and thus as the value of **randomStatistics**.

Note that there are several statements separated by semicolons. All these
statements together constitute a single "compound" statement, which is the
(single) second argument to **Module**. Whenever you have a sequence of
statements in a function, be *sure* to separate them with semicolons. Other-

wise *Mathematica* assumes that you mean to multiply them together (since blank space, including a line break, means multiplication).

Here is an example of what this function does:

```
randomStatistics[10]

Maximum = 0.918463
Minimum = 0.0169047
Average = 0.354447

{0.616932, 0.22935, 0.918463, 0.26326, 0.0180222,
   0.684887, 0.158835, 0.122851, 0.514969, 0.0169047}
```

Recursion is allowed in *Mathematica* function definitions. Often it is easiest to do recursion using pattern matching, so it will be discussed in Chapter 40, "How do I use patterns?".

We have described the fundamental elements needed to do procedural programming in *Mathematica*. There are many functions you can use to implement your programs. Here are the most important ones:

- **Table[expr, {var, min, max}]** evaluates **expr** repeatedly and saves up the results in a list, which it returns.

- **Map[f, list]** applies the function **f** to each element of **list**.

- **Do[expr, {var, min, max}]** evaluates **expr** repeatedly but does not save up the results. (**Do** is the most useful way of doing simple iteration.)

- **While[test, body]** evaluates **body** repeatedly as long as **test** returns **True** (**test** is checked before **body** is evaluated the first time).

- **If[test, truecase, falsecase]** evaluates **truecase** if **test** returns **True**, and **falsecase** if it returns **False**. If **test** returns anything else, the statement is left unevaluated. If you add a fourth argument to the **If**, that argument is evaluated if **test** returns neither **True** nor **False**.

- `lhs == rhs` returns **True** if the two sides are structurally identical and remains unevaluated otherwise. (The comparison is structural, not mathematical, so `Sin[x]^2 + Cos[x]^2 == 1` is not **True**. On the other hand, `a+b == b+a` is **True**, because the right-hand side is automatically sorted before the comparison.)

- `lhs === rhs` returns **True** if the two sides are identical, and **False** otherwise. (The comparison is the same as for `==`, except that `===` returns **False** instead of remaining unevaluated when the two sides are not identical.)

- `lhs != rhs` returns **False** if the two sides are identical, and remains unevaluated otherwise (`!=` means "not equal").

- `lhs =!= rhs` returns **False** if the two sides are identical, and **True** otherwise.

- `lhs > rhs` returns **True** if `lhs` is numerically greater than `rhs`, and remains unevaluated otherwise.

- `lhs < rhs` returns **True** if `lhs` is numerically less than `rhs`, and remains unevaluated otherwise.

- `lhs >= rhs` returns **True** if `lhs` is numerically greater than or equal to `rhs`, and remains unevaluated otherwise.

- `lhs <= rhs` returns **True** if `lhs` is numerically less than or equal to `rhs`, and remains unevaluated otherwise.

Although the functions **For**, **Goto**, **Return**, **Throw**, and **Catch** exist, their use is not recommended except for certain rare circumstances in which they are genuinely unavoidable.

There are a variety of ways to debug *Mathematica* programs. Since *Mathematica* is an interpreted language, you always have access to your variables and definitions in an interactive way. Tracing the flow of a program is a little harder, though. The most useful functions in this connection are **Print**, **Dialog**, and **Trace**.

Print can be used to print out the values of variables during the execution of a program, so you can see what is happening. For example, here is a program to draw polygons with a given number of sides:

```
drawPoly[n_] := Module[
    {list},

    list = Table[{Cos[t], Sin[t]}, {t,0,2Pi,2Pi/n}];

    Show[Graphics[Polygon[list]],
        AspectRatio -> Automatic];
]

drawPoly[7]
```

If we wanted to see what the value of **list** was during the execution of this function, we could insert a **Print** statement in the definition, like this:

```
drawPoly[n_] := Module[
    {list},

    list = Table[{Cos[t], Sin[t]}, {t,0,2Pi,2Pi/n}];

    Print[list];

    Show[Graphics[Polygon[list]],
        AspectRatio -> Automatic];
]

drawPoly[7]
```

$$\{\{1, 0\}, \{Cos[\frac{2 Pi}{7}], Sin[\frac{2 Pi}{7}]\}, \{Cos[\frac{4 Pi}{7}], Sin[\frac{4 Pi}{7}]$$

$$\{Cos[\frac{6 Pi}{7}], Sin[\frac{6 Pi}{7}]\}, \{Cos[\frac{8 Pi}{7}], Sin[\frac{8 Pi}{7}]\},$$

$$\{Cos[\frac{10 Pi}{7}], Sin[\frac{10 Pi}{7}]\}, \{Cos[\frac{12 Pi}{7}], Sin[\frac{12 Pi}{7}]\},$$

$$\{1, 0\}\}$$

Seeing the output might indicate to us that it would be a good idea to insert an **N** function in the **Table** command, to avoid building up a large symbolic table (which is slow):

```
drawPoly[n_] := Module[
   {list},

   list=Table[N[{Cos[t],Sin[t]}], {t,0,2Pi,2Pi/n}];

   Print[list];

   Show[Graphics[Polygon[list]],
      AspectRatio -> Automatic];
]
drawPoly[7]
{{1., 0}, {0.62349, 0.781831},

  {-0.222521, 0.974928}, {-0.900969, 0.433884},

  {-0.900969, -0.433884}, {-0.222521, -0.974928},

  {0.62349, -0.781831}, {1., 0}}
```

Once we had the definition right, we would remove the **Print** statement.

A different way to get the same information would be to insert a **Dialog** command instead of a **Print** command. When execution of the function reaches the **Dialog** command, execution will stop and we will enter *dialog mode*. In a Notebook version of *Mathematica*, the cell bracket of the cell being evaluated turns gray in dialog mode. In a raw terminal version a special dialog prompt is issued. (Note that the words Inspector and Dialog are used somewhat interchangeably in *Mathematica* documentation.)

Once we are in dialog mode, we can evaluate any expressions we want (for example, to find out the values of variables). When we exit dialog mode (either by choosing the Exit Dialog command from the Action menu in a Notebook version, or by evaluating **Return[]** in either a Notebook or raw terminal version), the main evaluation continues.

There is one slight complication to this. The way **Module** avoids name conflicts with local variables is by appending a serial number to each name you specify. So, for example, the variable **list** in the definitions above will, when it is used, be called something like **list$20**. It is a bit tricky to find out the actual name being used. A simple solution is to temporarily remove the names of the local variables from the first argument to **Module**. Here is the modified definition:

```
drawPoly[n_] := Module[
   {},

   list=Table[N[{Cos[t],Sin[t]}], {t,0,2Pi,2Pi/n}];

   Dialog[];

   Show[Graphics[Polygon[list]],
      AspectRatio -> Automatic];
]
```

Now we can try out the function:

```
drawPoly[7]
```

No output is produced at first, but the cell bracket of the cell containing **drawPoly[7]** is in gray, indicating that we are in dialog mode:

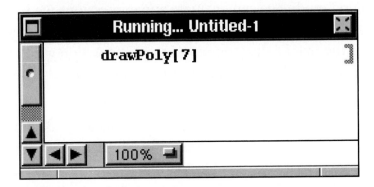

We can now ask for the value of **list** by evaluating the following expression:

```
list
{{1., 0}, {0.62349, 0.781831},
   {-0.222521, 0.974928}, {-0.900969, 0.433884},
   {-0.900969, -0.433884}, {-0.222521, -0.974928},
   {0.62349, -0.781831}, {1., 0}}
```

If this were a more complicated function, we could evaluate a variety of different expressions to learn what was going on. We could also change the value of variables, although this can sometimes be quite confusing. When we are done, we choose Exit Dialog from the Action menu to continue with the main evaluation, at which point the output is produced:

Normally the output would be placed right below the cell being evaluated, but we've separated it here for clarity.

There are several ways of entering dialog mode. We've just seen how to do it by placing a **Dialog** command at a specific location in a function. A second way is to interrupt a running calculation using the Interrupt Calculation command in the Action menu (or typing Command-Comma) in a Notebook version, or typing Control-C in a raw terminal version. This will bring up the Interrupt options panel, one of whose choices is Enter Dialog. Since you can't tell exactly where the interrupt will stop the calculation, this is a somewhat haphazard way of seeing what is happening. On the other hand, if you have a program with one long loop, this can be a good way to find out how far it's gotten after you lose patience. A dialog entered this way can be exited the same way as one entered with the **Dialog** command.

A third way to enter a dialog is to use the Evaluate In Dialog command in the Action menu. (This command is not available in raw terminal versions). Evaluate In Dialog, which can be used only when another calculation is running, automatically interrupts the calculation, enters dialog mode, evaluates the selected cell or cells, and then exits the dialog. This is useful to find out the instantaneous value of an expression without stopping the main calculation any longer than necessary. A shortcut for Evaluate In Dialog is Shift-Option-Return.

Trace is perhaps the most powerful debugging tool, but its proper use requires practice. First we will restore the definition of **drawPoly** to its original form:

```
drawPoly[n_] := Module[
   {list},

   list=Table[N[{Cos[t],Sin[t]}], {t,0,2Pi,2Pi/n}];

   Show[Graphics[Polygon[list]],
      AspectRatio -> Automatic];
]
```

Now we can apply **Trace** to it:

```
Trace[drawPoly[3], list]
```

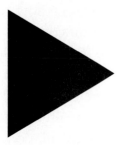

```
{{{{{list$36, {{1., 0}, {-0.5, 0.866025},
       {-0.5, -0.866025}, {1., 0}}}}}}}
```

In this form, the first argument is the expression to be evaluated and the second argument is a symbol name. All transformation rules involving the symbol **list** will be accumulated into the output of the **Trace** command. In this case there was only one, the the assignment to **list**.

The power of **Trace** lies in its second argument. That argument can be either a symbol name (in which case the output of **Trace** will be a list of all the expressions involving that symbol), or it can be a *Mathematica* pattern (in which case the output will be a list of all the expressions matching the pattern). The latter form allows very selective display of the flow of evaluation.

Advanced readers are advised to read about **Trace** in The *Mathematica* Book.

Chapter 39
Should I *ever* use a **For** loop?

If you go to a fancy university and take a fancy programming class, they will tell you that commands such as "for", "goto", and "return" are amateurish and old fashioned. They are, of course, right. With a proper modern language, using these commands is never necessary and is rarely a good idea. There are alternatives that are more efficient, easier to understand, and less likely to cause confusion.

The following example of *Mathematica* code was found in a manuscript from an author who shall remain nameless:

```
list2 = {};
For[i = 1, i <= Length[list1], ++i,
   AppendTo[list2, Sin[ list1[[i]] ]]
]
```

After some consideration, it is possible to determine that this statement builds up a list (**list2**) that contains the sine of each element of **list1**. The following command does *exactly* the same thing:

```
list2 = Sin[list1]
```

The **Sin** function has the attribute **Listable**, which means that, when it's applied to a list, it is automatically applied to each element in the list. Here's a specific example:

```
Sin[{1, 2, 3, 4}]
{Sin[1], Sin[2], Sin[3], Sin[4]}
```

The **Listable** attribute is one of the features of *Mathematica* in which iteration over elements in a list is done automatically for you, without the need for an explicit loop. Let's explore **Listable** in more detail.

Most built-in functions for which it makes sense have the **Listable** attribute, so it's easy to apply them to lists. The following (rather intimidating) piece of *Mathematica* code generates a list of all the built-in listable functions (don't worry about understanding the code, we just want to look at the list):

```
TableForm[Transpose[Partition[Map[
    First,
    Select[
      Map[{#, Attributes[#]}&, Names["*"]],
      ( !FreeQ[#, Listable])&
]], 47]]]
```

Abs	EllipticPi	MessageList
AiryAi	EllipticTheta	Minus
AiryAiPrime	EllipticThetaPrime	Mod
AiryBi	Erf	N
AiryBiPrime	Erfc	Negative
ArcCos	Erfi	NonNegative
ArcCosh	EulerPhi	$NumberBits
ArcCot	EvenQ	OddQ
ArcCoth	Exp	Out
ArcCsc	ExpIntegralE	Plus
ArcCsch	ExpIntegralEi	Pochhammer
ArcSec	Exponent	PolyGamma
ArcSech	Factorial	PolyLog
ArcSin	Factorial2	PolynomialGCD
ArcSinh	FactorInteger	PolynomialLCM
ArcTan	Floor	Positive
ArcTanh	FresnelC	Power
Arg	FresnelS	PowerMod
ArithmeticGeometricMean	Gamma	Prime
Attributes	GammaRegularized	PrimeQ
BesselI	GCD	Quotient
BesselJ	GegenbauerC	Range
BesselK	HermiteH	Re
BesselY	HypergeometricU	RealDigits
Beta	Hypergeometric0F1	Resultant
BetaRegularized	Hypergeometric0F1Regularized	RiemannSiegelTheta
Binomial	Hypergeometric1F1	RiemannSiegelZ
Cancel	Hypergeometric1F1Regularized	Round
Ceiling	Hypergeometric2F1	Sec
Characters	Hypergeometric2F1Regularized	Sech
ChebyshevT	Im	SetAccuracy
ChebyshevU	In	SetPrecision
Conjugate	InString	Sign
Cos	IntegerDigits	Sin
Cosh	JacobiP	Sinh
CoshIntegral	JacobiSymbol	SinhIntegral
CosIntegral	JacobiZeta	SinIntegral
Cot	LaguerreL	SphericalHarmonicY
Coth	LCM	Sqrt
Csc	LegendreP	Subtract
Csch	LegendreQ	Tan
Divide	LerchPhi	Tanh
Divisors	Limit	Times
DivisorSigma	Log	ToExpression
EllipticE	LogGamma	Together
EllipticF	LogIntegral	ToHeldExpression
EllipticK	MantissaExponent	Zeta

Listability also works for functions with more than one argument (for example, **Mod**). Here is an example of **Mod** applied to two numbers:

```
Mod[10, 3]
```

```
1
```

The result, 1, is 10 modulo 3 (the remainder after dividing 10 by 3). If you have several numbers and you want to see what each of them is modulo the same number, you can give **Mod** a list as its first argument:

```
Mod[{10, 11, 12, 13, 14}, 3]
```

```
{1, 2, 0, 1, 2}
```

Conversely, if you have a number and you want to see what it is modulo several other numbers, you can give **Mod** a list as its second argument:

```
Mod[10, {3, 4, 5, 6, 7}]
```

```
{1, 2, 0, 4, 3}
```

If you have several numbers and you want to see each of them modulo a different number, you can give **Mod** two lists:

```
Mod[{10, 11, 12, 13, 14}, {3, 4, 5, 6, 7}]
```

```
{1, 3, 2, 1, 0}
```

If you are using two lists, as we have just done, they must be the same length; otherwise they can't be matched element by element:

```
Mod[{10, 11, 12, 13, 14}, {3, 4, 5}]
```

```
Thread::tdlen:
    Objects of unequal length in
      Mod[{10, 11, 12, 13, 14}, {3, 4, 5}]
      cannot be combined.
Mod[{10, 11, 12, 13, 14}, {3, 4, 5}]
```

If you define your own function and then want to apply it to a list, you can either give it the **Listable** attribute or use the **Map** function:

```
Map[f, {1, 2, 3}]
{f[1], f[2], f[3]}
```

Or:

```
Attributes[f] = {Listable};
f[{1, 2, 3}]
{f[1], f[2], f[3]}
```

You can think of the **Listable** attribute as meaning that the function will automatically invoke the **Map** command whenever it is applied to a list. For functions with more than one argument, the corresponding command that is automatically applied is called **Thread**. This command is beyond the scope of this book.

People are also tempted to use the **For** command when they want a table of numbers. For example, the following code will build up a table of squares:

```
list = {};
For[i = 1, i <= 10, ++i,
   AppendTo[list, i^2]
];
list
{1, 4, 9, 16, 25, 36, 49, 64, 81, 100}
```

This code is hard to understand and runs quite slowly. The following command generates the same list:

```
Table[i^2, {i, 1, 10}]
{1, 4, 9, 16, 25, 36, 49, 64, 81, 100}
```

This **Table** command is easier to understand than the **For** loop, particularly if one is familiar with the iterator form **{variable, start, end}**, which is commonly used in *Mathematica*.

The examples above all involve list manipulation. In *Mathematica* there are many commands for dealing with lists without the need for explicit loops. Chapter 13, "What are lists and what can I do with them?", explains some of these functions.

Sometimes you do need an actual loop, but that doesn't mean that **For** is the best choice. The following example prints Hello five times:

```
For[i = 1, i <= 5, ++i, Print["Hello"]]
Hello
Hello
Hello
Hello
Hello
```

Now consider this command:

```
Do[Print["Hello"], {i, 1, 5}]
Hello
Hello
Hello
Hello
Hello
```

Notice that the syntax of **Do** is very similar to that of **Table** (identical, in fact). This sort of consistency makes it easy to remember how to use commands.

Since we don't use the variable **i** anywhere in the body of this loop, we can actually use an abbreviated form of the **Do** loop:

```
Do[Print["Hello"], {5}]
Hello
Hello
Hello
Hello
Hello
```

In many cases, **Do** provides a very clear and efficient way to do a fixed-length loop. In cases where you need a more complicated stopping condition, the **While** command may be a good choice. See The *Mathematica* Book for more information about these commands.

Chapter 40
How do I use patterns?

Mathematica's pattern matcher is perhaps the feature that most distinguish-es it from other symbolic mathematics programs. Pattern matching can be used in a startling variety of ways and is fundamental to almost anything you do in *Mathematica*.

Let's start by seeing how patterns can be used to transform expressions. Here is an expression:

    a + b

    a + b

We can use the substitute operator (**/.**) along with a replacement rule (**->**) to substitute a new expression for **b**:

    a + b /. b -> x^2

    a + x²

The **/.** operator should be read "replace" and **->** should be read "with". The whole expressions is "in **a + b** replace **b** with **x^2**".

In this example, the **b** in the replacement rule is a pattern. It is a simple pattern, in that it only matches a literal "b". Let's try a more complicated expression:

    a + log[E^x]

    a + log[E^x]

We could simplify by canceling the log with the power:

```
a + log[E^x] /. log[E^x] -> x
```

a + x

In this case, **log[E^x]** is a somewhat more complicated pattern: *Mathematica* compares it with the expression to find what subpart of the expression matches the pattern.

Both the patterns we've seen are literal patterns. That is, they match one and only one possible expression. For example, the following does not work:

```
a + log[E^y] /. log[E^x] -> x
```

a + log[E^y]

Since the pattern matches only expressions involving **x**, it does not match **log[E^y]**. If we want to write a pattern that matches **log[E^***anything***]**, we can use an underscore (_). The pattern **log[E^n_]** means "match any expression of this form, regardless of what **n_** is":

```
a + log[E^y] /. log[E^n_] -> n
```

a + y

Here are some more examples of expressions that match this pattern:

```
a + log[E^(x+y)] /. log[E^n_] -> n
```

a + x + y

```
a + log[E^Sin[x+y]] /. log[E^n_] -> n
```

a + Sin[x + y]

In each case, *Mathematica* figured out what **n_** needed to be to match the pattern and used that value as the replacement.

You can write patterns with more than one underscore:

```
x + Sin[a + b] /.
      Sin[n_ + m_] -> Cos[n] Sin[m] + Cos[m] Sin[n]
```

```
x + Cos[b] Sin[a] + Cos[a] Sin[b]
```

Let's consider this more complicated expression:

```
Cos[x]+Cos[x]^2+Sin[x]+Sin[x]^2
```

$$Cos[x] + Cos[x]^2 + Sin[x] + Sin[x]^2$$

It could be simplified using the identity "sine squared plus cosine squared equals one". We could write this using a literal pattern:

```
Cos[x]+Cos[x]^2+Sin[x]+Sin[x]^2 /.
              Sin[x]^2+Cos[x]^2 -> 1
```

```
1 + Cos[x] + Sin[x]
```

Notice that *Mathematica* had to reorder the addition to make this pattern match. Later we'll learn more about what kinds of rearrangements *Mathematica* will do to get a pattern to match.

A literal pattern, however, is not a very satisfactory way to do this transformation. We want to write a pattern that matches **Sin[**anything**]^2 + Cos[**anything**]^2** with the further restriction that both anythings must be the same. This can be done by using a pattern with two underscores, both with the same name:

```
Cos[x]+Cos[x]^2+Sin[x]+Sin[x]^2 /.
              Sin[n_]^2+Cos[n_]^2 -> 1
```

```
1 + Cos[x] + Sin[x]
```

In the following example, this pattern matches one pair but not the other:

```
Cos[a]^2+Cos[x]^2+Sin[a]^2+Sin[y]^2 /.
              Sin[n_]^2+Cos[n_]^2 -> 1
```

$$1 + Cos[x]^2 + Sin[y]^2$$

If you are not at least slightly amazed at this example, consider rereading it.

So far we have been applying pattern transformations manually to individual expressions. It is also possible to enter such transformations into the global rule base so they are applied automatically whenever an expression is evaluated. This is called *assignment*.

For example, the following assignment adds a pattern transformation rule to the global rule base:

```
h = 5
```
5

The pattern in this case is the literal **h**. Now, anytime we evaluate an expression involving **h**, the value **5** will be substituted:

```
h^2
```
25

Note that this is exactly the same as if we had applied the transformation manually:

```
h^2 /. h -> 5
```
25

So we see that assigning a value to a variable is really the same thing as writing a transformation rule and adding it to the global rule base. (Internally, *Mathematica* actually implements it this way.)

We can add a more complicated rule such as the one we were looking at earlier:

```
log[E^n_] = n
```
n

Now we don't have to apply any rules manually:

```
a + log[E^y]
```

a + y

```
a + log[E^(x+y)]
```

a + x + y

```
a + log[E^Sin[x+y]]
```

a + Sin[x + y]

Just like variable definitions, function definitions are also patterns. For example, here is a pattern rule that implements a function:

```
square[n_] = n^2
```

n^2

This patterns says **square[** *anything* **]** is to be transformed into *anything* squared. This is just what a function should do, and indeed we can use **square** like any other function:

```
square[5]
```

25

In fact, *all* functions in *Mathematica* are defined in much this way.

There is one further complication. Consider the following example:

```
expanding[n_] = Expand[(a+b)^n]
```

$(a + b)^n$

Let's use it:

```
expanding[5]
```

$(a + b)^5$

The problem is that the **Expand** function was evaluated at the time the definition was made, before **n** had any specific numerical value. It returned the expression unexpanded, and this resulting expression became part of the rule. What we want instead is to have the *unevaluated* **Expand** expression become part of the rule. This is done using :=instead of =.

```
expanding[n_] := Expand[(a+b)^n]
```

Let's use this new version:

```
expanding[5]
```

$$a^5 + 5 a^4 b + 10 a^3 b^2 + 10 a^2 b^3 + 5 a b^4 + b^5$$

It's usually the case that if you have an _ on the left-hand side of the definition, then you want to use delayed assignment (:=). Otherwise you want to use immediate assignment (=). This is because _'s on the left-hand side mean that there are variables on the right-hand side that are going to take on different values when the definition is used.

Since function definitions are patterns, we are not restricted to functions that take just one or more arguments. We can define functions that automatically "recognize" patterns and transform them. We can even make multiple definitions for the same function so it can do different things to different patterns.

For example, here is a function that, when applied to a single number, returns its absolute value, but when applied to a list of two numbers (a vector) returns the length of the vector (this is like a generalized velocity function that works in both one and two dimensions):

```
velocity[n_] := Abs[n]
velocity[{x_, y_}] := Sqrt[x^2 + y^2]
```

Here is how it works in each case:

```
velocity[-3]
```

3

```
velocity[{3, 5}]
```

Sqrt[34]

The reader may notice that there is a complication here: The first definition is for **velocity**[*anything*]. When **velocity** is applied to a list of two elements, it could match either rule because, after all, a list of two elements is an *anything*. This problem is dealt with in *Mathematica* by automatically arranging the rules in order of increasing generality. Since the second definition is more specific than the first, it is tried first. (This ordering is not always completely determined, nor does it always work as intended. The problem is a deep and subtle one about which tomes are written. *Mathematica's* solution is expedient, but not perfect.)

Recursion is another example in which having multiple definitions for the same function is useful. Any time you evaluate an expression, *Mathematica* applies all the rules it has once. Then it applies them again, and again, and so on until the expression stops changing. So if you have a rule that transforms an expression into another expression to which the same rule can also be applied, it will be applied again and again (potentially forever).

Consider the classic definition of the factorial function:

```
fac[n_] := n fac[n-1]
```

This says, **fac**[*anything*] is *anything* times **fac** of one less than *anything*. This is fine, except that it is an infinite loop: It will never stop. We need to add a special case that allows the recursion to come to an end. The usual way is to say that **fac[0]** is 1:

```
fac[0] = 1
```
```
1
```

Now we can use the definition:

```
fac[10]
```
```
3628800
```

The first rule was used 10 times and the second rule once. Although a factorial function could be written without using patterns in this way, the definition would not be nearly as neat and easy to understand.

We mentioned earlier that *Mathematica* sometimes has to reorder expressions to get a pattern to match. Consider this example:

```
a + b + c + d /. a + d -> x
b + c + x
```

Mathematica had to try several reorderings of the addition before it could notice that **a** and **d** could be brought together, thereby matching the pattern.

On the other hand, consider this example:

```
(a + b) c /. a c -> x
(a + b) c
```

Mathematica did *not* notice that it could have rewritten the expression as **a c + b c** and then applied the rule.

When will *Mathematica* reorganize an expression? There are only two specific things *Mathematica* will do to try to match an expression. First, it will change the order of commutative functions (like addition and multiplication). Second, it will try different groupings of associative functions (like addition and multiplication).

It will never try any structural rearrangements (like expanding, factoring, distributing, etc.). That is, patterns in *Mathematica* are strictly structural, not mathematical or algebraic. Two expressions may be mathematically identical (like **a (b+c)** and **a b + a c**), but they are not structurally identical, and *Mathematica* will not match them as patterns.

There are objects called **AlgebraicRules** that can be used to carry out true algebraic transformations, but their use is beyond the scope of this book. The reader is advised to consult The *Mathematica* Book for information about **AlgebraicRules** as well as for information about the many additional features available for structural pattern matching.

■ Worked Example

We'll write a set of rules to expand any trigonometric expression into the lowest possible angle. That is, if we see **Sin[2 a]**, we want to write in a form involving only **Sin[a]** and **Cos[a]**. (This is for educational purposes only: There are built-in *Mathematica* functions to do this, like **Factor**, **Expand**, **Apart**, and **Together** with the option **Trig->True**. See The *Mathematica* Book for more information.)

Since we don't want any conflicts with the built-in **Sin** and **Cos** functions, we'll write all our rules in terms of **sin** and **cos** instead. The lowercase first letter will distinguish our functions from the built-in ones.

First we write the formulas for the sum of two angles:

```
sin[a_ + b_] := cos[a] sin[b] + cos[b] sin[a]

cos[a_ + b_] := cos[a] cos[b] - sin[a] sin[b]
```

Next we want to write the rule for integer multiples of angles. If we have, for example, **sin[3x]**, we can write this as **sin[x + 2x]** and then use one of the added angle formulas for addition. More generally, **sin[n   x]** can be written as **sin[x + (n-1)x]**.

Our first attempt to write the rule might be:

```
sin[n_ a_]:=cos[a] sin[(n-1) a]+cos[(n-1) a] sin[a]
```

This is just like the rule for **sin[a + b]**, with **b** being **(n-1) a**.

Here we run into some complications that will require learning about new types of patterns. This pattern matches **sin[***anything* times *anything-else***]**. The problem is that we treat the **n** and the **a** differently: **n** must be an integer for the formula to work. When a rule like the one above is applied to, say, **sin[5 x]**, we can't be sure whether it will match **5** with **n** and **x** with **a**, or the reverse (since multiplication is commutative).

We need to tell *Mathematica* that **n** must be an integer for the pattern to match. This is done by using **n_Integer** instead of **n_**. The pattern **n_Integer** matches anything that is an integer. (Technically, it matches any expression whose "Head" is **Integer**. The *Mathematica* Book explains in detail what this means.)

The improved rule is:

```
sin[n_Integer a_] :=
      cos[a] sin[(n-1) a] + cos[(n-1) a] sin[a]
```

But there is still a problem. If **n** is a negative integer, this rule will go into an infinite loop. We need to add another condition that says this rule applies only if **n** is positive.

We can add a condition to any rule by appending a **/;** clause at the end:

```
sin[n_Integer a_] :=
    cos[a] sin[(n-1) a] + cos[(n-1) a] sin[a] /;
                        Positive[n]
```

Positive is a function that returns **True** or **False** depending on whether or not its argument is positive. You can add arbitrarily complicated conditions to a rule, as long as they return **True** or **False** in the end.

If your condition is a single function of one argument, you can use a shortcut and write the same rule like this:

```
sin[n_Integer?Positive a_] :=
    cos[a] sin[(n-1) a] + cos[(n-1) a] sin[a]
```

You may wonder why there are two different ways to specify conditions. That is, why does the **Integer** go right after the **_**, and the **Positive** after a question mark? This is a somewhat complicated issue, and it mainly concerns efficiency. If you like, you can write all the conditions in the **/;** clause like this:

```
sin[n_ a_] :=
    cos[a] sin[(n-1) a] + cos[(n-1) a] sin[a] /;
                (IntegerQ[n] && Positive[n])
```

The *Mathematica* Book explains these issues in great detail. We'll use the shorter form for now.

Using what we've learned, we can write the multiple angle rules for **sin** and **cos**:

```
sin[n_Integer?Positive a_] :=
    cos[a] sin[(n-1) a] + cos[(n-1) a] sin[a]

cos[n_Integer?Positive a_] :=
    cos[a] cos[(n-1) a] - sin[a] sin[(n-1) a]
```

What about negative integers? We can write two more rules that turn negative integers into positive ones:

```
sin[n_Integer?Negative a_] := -sin[-n a]

cos[n_Integer?Negative a_] := cos[-n a]
```

Here, together in one place, are all the rules we've developed. We've added **Expand** to the multiple angle formulas because it makes the answer come out nicer looking.

```
sin[a_ + b_] := cos[a] sin[b] + cos[b] sin[a]
cos[a_ + b_] := cos[a] cos[b] - sin[a] sin[b]
sin[n_Integer?Negative a_] := -sin[-n a]
cos[n_Integer?Negative a_] := cos[-n a]
sin[n_Integer?Positive a_] :=
    Expand[cos[a] sin[(n-1) a] + cos[(n-1) a] sin[a]]
cos[n_Integer?Positive a_] :=
    Expand[cos[a] cos[(n-1) a] - sin[a] sin[(n-1) a]]
```

Let's try them out on a few examples:

```
sin[x + y]
cos[y] sin[x] + cos[x] sin[y]

sin[2 x]
2 cos[x] sin[x]
```

```
cos[4 x]
```

$$\cos[x]^4 - 6 \cos[x]^2 \sin[x]^2 + \sin[x]^4$$

```
sin[2 x - 5 y]
```

$$2 \cos[x] \sin[x] (\cos[y]^5 - 10 \cos[y]^3 \sin[y]^2 +$$
$$5 \cos[y] \sin[y]^4) +$$
$$(\cos[x]^2 - \sin[x]^2) (-5 \cos[y]^4 \sin[y] +$$
$$10 \cos[y]^2 \sin[y]^3 - \sin[y]^5)$$

In this last example we can see that the rules all work together, even if they have to be applied several times before the answer is reduced to lowest possible terms.

◼ Worked Example

We might want to define a function that calculates the distance between two points in two dimensions. We could do this by defining a function with four arguments:

```
distance[x1_, y1_, x2_, y2_] :=
    Sqrt[(x2 - x1)^2 + (y2 - y1)^2]
```

We can use this on the points (3, 7) and (6, 2):

```
distance[3, 7, 6, 2]
```
```
Sqrt[34]
```

This is not the best way to define the function. In *Mathematica*, points are usually represented as lists of two numbers. For example, we might assign the variable **pointA** to hold our first point, and **pointB** to hold our second point:

```
pointA = {3, 7};
pointB = {6, 2};
```

We can't use our distance function directly on these two points, because our function takes four arguments, not two. That is, we can't say:

```
distance[pointA, pointB]
```

Instead we would have to say:

```
distance[pointA[[1]], pointA[[2]],
     pointB[[1]], pointB[[2]]]
```

```
Sqrt[34]
```

The notation **pointA[[1]]** means the first element of **pointA**.

This is very ugly. Instead, we might define **distance** in such a way that it takes two lists as arguments. We could define it this way:

```
betterDistance[pA_, pB_] :=
    Sqrt[(pB[[1]]-pA[[1]])^2 + (pB[[2]]-pA[[2]])^2]
```

This can be used on our point variables:

```
betterDistance[pointA, pointB]
```

```
Sqrt[34]
```

But the definition is still rather ugly. Let's try a pattern definition to "pick out" the elements of the lists automatically:

```
evenBetterDistance[{x1_, y1_}, {x2_, y2_}] :=
    Sqrt[(x2 - x1)^2 + (y2 - y1)^2]
```

This function can be used on our point variables:

```
evenBetterDistance[point1, point2]
```

```
Sqrt[34]
```

Or we can enter the points directly:

```
evenBetterDistance[{3, 7}, {6, 2}]
```

```
Sqrt[34]
```

References

Following are the books currently available about *Mathematica*. Many can be found in technical bookstores. They can also be ordered directly from their publishers or distributors (see below for phone numbers).

Mathematica: A Practical Approach, Nancy Blachman (Prentice-Hall, 1991).

Mathematica: Quick Reference, Nancy Blachman (Variable Symbols, 1990).

Calculus & Mathematica, Part 1, Don Brown, Horacio Porta, and Jerry Uhl (Addison-Wesley, 1991).

Mathematica for the Sciences, Richard Crandall (Addison-Wesley, 1991).

A Guidebook to Calculus and Mathematica, P. Crooke and J. Ratcliffe (Wadsworth Publishing, 1991).

Calculus & Mathematica, Part 2, William Davis, J. Manton, Horacio Porta, and Jerry Uhl (Addison-Wesley, 1991).

A Tutorial Introduction to Mathematica, Wade Ellis and Ed Lodi (Brooks/Cole, 1991).

Exploring Mathematics with Mathematica, Theodore W. Gray and Jerry Glynn (Addison-Wesley, 1991). Distributed by MathWare.

Programming in Mathematica, Second Edition, Roman Maeder (Addison-Wesley, 1991).

Implementing Discrete Mathematics: Combinatorics and Graph Theory with Mathematica, Steven Skiena (Addison-Wesley, 1991).

Computational Recreations in Mathematica, Ilan Vardi (Addison-Wesley, 1991).

Mathematica in Action, Stan Wagon (W.H. Freeman, 1991).

Mathematica: A System for Doing Mathematics by Computer, Second Edition, Stephen Wolfram (Addison-Wesley, 1991).

Guide to Standard Packages, (Wolfram Research, Inc., 1991). Available only as part of *Mathematica* Version 2.

Elementary Tutorial Notes, (Wolfram Research, Inc., 1991).

Intermediate Tutorial Notes, (Wolfram Research, Inc., 1991).

Advanced Tutorial Notes, (Wolfram Research, Inc., 1991).

The Mathematica Journal, (Addison-Wesley, quarterly).

Following are phone numbers for the publishers referred to above:

Addison-Wesley, 800-447-2226

Brooks/Cole, 800-354-9706

W.H. Freeman, 801-973-4660

MathWare, 800-255-2468

Variable Symbols, 510-843-8701

Wadsworth Publishing, 800-354-9706

Wolfram Research, 217-398-0700

Index